THE OFFICIAL **NATIONAL PARK GUIDE**

SNOWDONIA

Text by Merfyn Williams · Photographs by Jeremy Moore

SERIES EDITOR **Roly Smith**

PEVENSEY GUIDES

The author wishes to thank
Snowdonia National Park staff,
especially Barbara Jones and Peter
Ogden for their help and support,
and also Wil Jones, Croesor, for
advice on the chapter on wildlife.

The Pevensey Press is an imprint of
David & Charles

First published in the UK in 2000

Map artwork by Chartwell Illustrators

Text copyright © Merfyn Williams 2000
Photographs copyright © Jeremy Moore 2000

Merfyn Williams has asserted his right to be
identified as author of this work in accordance
with the Copyright, Designs and Patents Act,
1988.

A catalogue record for this book is available
from the British Library.

ISBN 1 898630 13 5 (paperback)
ISBN 1 898630 22 4 (hardback)

Book design by
Les Dominey Design Company, Exeter
and printed in China by
Hong Kong Graphic & Printing Limited
for David & Charles
Brunel House   Newton Abbot   Devon

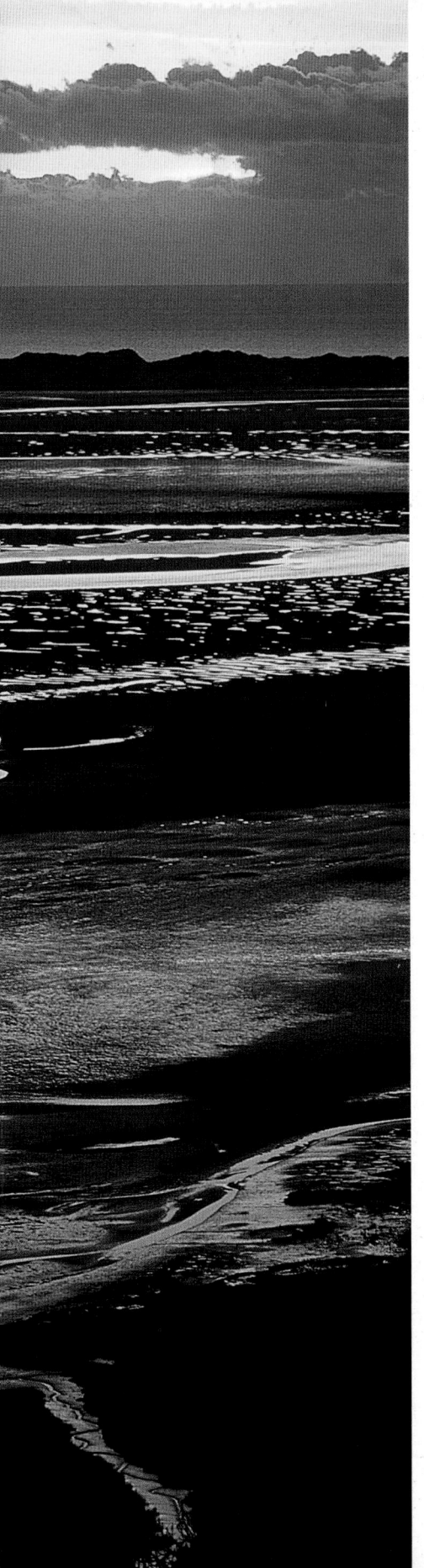

Contents

Page I: Pen yr Ole Wen

Pages 2–3: The magnificent Mawddach estuary, described more than once as the most beautiful place on earth. The Barmouth viaduct carries the Cambrian Coast railway line from Machynlleth to Pwllheli

Left: The shifting sandbanks of the Dyfi estuary – southern boundary of the National Park. The Dyfi is a National Nature Reserve which also includes the sand dunes at Ynyslas (pictured) on the Ceredigion side of the river

Front cover: (above) Aberglaslyn Pass; (below) Harlech Castle; (front flap) Mawddach Estuary
Back cover: (above) Cader Idris; (below) Snowdon and Llyn Mymbyr near Capel Curig

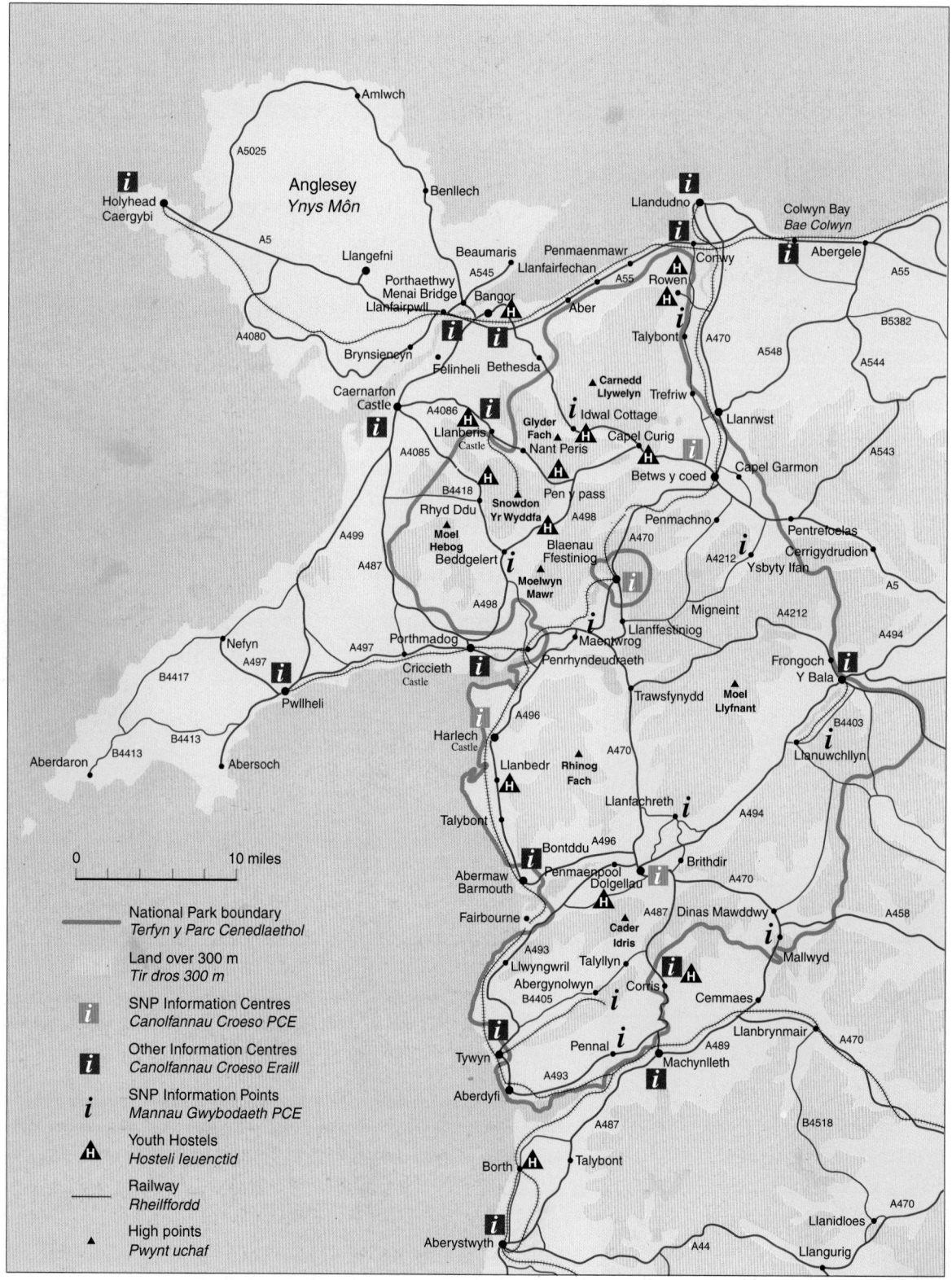

Amlwch

A5025

Anglesey
Ynys Môn

Benllech

Holyhead
Caergybi

A5

Llangefni

Beaumaris

Penmaenmawr

Llandudno

Colwyn Bay
Bae Colwyn

Abergele

A55

B5382

A544

Conwy

Rowen

Talybont

A470

A548

Porthaethwy
Menai Bridge
Llanfairpwll

Bangor

Aber

A545
Llanfairfechan

A55

Brynsieneyn

A4080

Felinheli

Bethesda

Carnedd
Llywelyn

Trefriw

Llanrwst

A543

Caernarfon
Castle

A4086

Idwal Cottage

Capel Garmon

Glyder
Fach

Llanberis
Castle

A4085

Nant Peris

Capel Curig

Betws y coed

Pentrefoelas

A5

B4418

Pen y pass

Penmachno

A4212

Ysbyty Ifan

Cerrigydrudion

Rhyd Ddu

Snowdon
Yr Wyddfa

A498

A470

A4212

Moel
Hebog

Beddgelert

Moelwyn
Mawr

Blaenau
Ffestiniog

Migneint

A4212

A494

A499

A487

A498

Llanffestiniog

Frongoch
Y Bala

Nefyn

A497

Porthmadog

Maentwrog

Trawsfynydd

Moel
Llyfnant

B4403

B4417

Criccieth
Castle

Penrhyndeudraeth

A470

Llanuwchllyn

Pwllheli

B4413

Harlech
Castle

A496

A470

Aberdaron

B4413

Abersoch

Llanbedr

Rhinog
Fach

Llanfachreth

A494

Talybont

A496

Bontddu

Brithdir

A470

Abermaw
Barmouth

Penmaenpool
Dolgellau

Dinas Mawddwy

A458

Fairbourne

Cader
Idris

A487

Mallwyd

Llwyngwril

Talyllyn

A493

Abergynolwyn

Corris

Cemmaes

B4405

Llanbrynmair

A470

Tywyn

Pennal

A489

Machynlleth

A493

Aberdyfi

A487

B4518

Borth

Talybont

Llanidloes

Aberystwyth

A44

Llangurig

A470

0   10 miles

National Park boundary
Terfyn y Parc Cenedlaethol

Land over 300 m
Tir dros 300 m

SNP Information Centres
Canolfannau Croeso PCE

Other Information Centres
Canolfannau Croeso Eraill

SNP Information Points
Mannau Gwybodaeth PCE

Youth Hostels
Hosteli Ieuenctid

Railway
Rheilffordd

High points
Pwynt uchaf

Foreword

by Professor Ian Mercer CBE, Secretary General, Association of National Park Authorities

The National Parks of Great Britain are very special places. Their landscapes include the most remote and dramatic hills and coasts in England and Wales, as well as the wild wetlands of the Broads. They still support the farming communities which have fashioned their detail over the centuries. They form the highest rank of the protected areas which society put in place in 1949. So, 1999 saw the fiftieth anniversary of the founding legislation which, incidentally, provided for Areas of Outstanding Natural Beauty, Nature Reserves, Areas of Special Scientific Interest and Long Distance Footpaths, as well as for National Parks.

In the eight years following that, ten Parks were designated. The Lake District, the Peak, Snowdonia and Dartmoor were already well visited, as were the North York Moors, Pembrokeshire Coast, Yorkshire Dales and Exmoor which quickly followed. The Brecon Beacons and Northumberland had their devotees too, though perhaps in lesser numbers then. The special quality of each of these places was already well known, and while those involved may not have predicted the numbers, mobility or aspirations of visitors accurately, the foresight of the landscape protection system cannot be too highly praised.

That system has had to evolve – not just to accommodate visitor numbers, but to meet the pressures flowing from agricultural change, hunger for housing and roadstone, thirst for water, and military manoeuvring – and indeed, the Norfolk and Suffolk Broads were added to the list in 1989. National Parks are now cared for by free-standing authorities who control development, hold land, grant-aid farmers and others, provide wardens, information, car parks and loos, clear footpaths and litter, plant trees and partner many other agents in pursuit of the purposes for which National Parks exist. Those purposes are paramount for all public agencies' consideration when they act within the Parks. They are:

- the conservation of the natural beauty, wildlife and cultural heritage of the area, and
- the promotion of the understanding and enjoyment of its special qualities by the public.

The National Park Authorities must, in pursuing those purposes, foster social and economic well-being. They now bring in some £48 million a year between them to be deployed in the Parks, in addition to normal local public spending.

This book is first a celebration of the National Park, of all its special qualities and of the people whose predecessors produced and maintained the detail of its character. The series to which this book belongs celebrates too the first fifty years of National Park protection in the United Kingdom, the foresight of the founding fathers, and the contributions since of individuals like John Sandford, Reg Hookway and Ron Edwards. The book and the series also mark the work of the present National Park Authorities and their staff, at the beginning of the next fifty years, and of the third millennium of historic time. Their dedication to their Parks is only matched by their aspiration for the sustainable enhancement of the living landscapes for which they are responsible. They need, and hope for, your support.

In the new century, national assets will only be properly maintained if the national will to conserve them is made manifest to national governments. I hope this book will whet your appetite for the National Park, or help you get more from your visit, and provoke you to use your democratic influence on its behalf. In any case it will remind you of the glories of one of the jewels in Britain's landscape crown. Do enjoy it.

Introducing Snowdonia

Where and what is 'Eryri'? Eryri is the Welsh name for Snowdonia and usually translated from 'eryr' meaning eagle and thus apparently means the place of the eagles. But as with many descriptive names in Wales, the obvious derivation is not necessarily the correct one, and the name actually originates from a Medieval Welsh word 'eryr' meaning a high place. Thus the first lesson we must learn is that things are hardly ever what they seem in Eryri.

To the people of the area, Eryri means the area centred on its grandest mountain, Snowdon or Yr Wyddfa. Yr Wyddfa originates from 'Gwyddfa', which is an old Welsh word for monument and it is the burial place of the giant Rita Gawr. Eryri, therefore, is Yr Wyddfa and her family surrounded by cousins and friends such as the mountains of the Glyder and the Carneddau interspersed with the dramatic valleys of Ogwen, Peris and Nant Gwynant. These are at the north-western edge of the Snowdonia National Park. The northern extremity reaches to the Menai Strait east of Bangor, follows the Conwy Valley south to Betws y Coed and then west to near Porthmadog and back north towards Caernarfon. The raw material of their creation was the product of unimaginable volcanic eruptions some 300 million years ago.

But the Snowdonia National Park is much more extensive than the northern core of Eryri. In fact, most of the 827sq miles (2,142sq km) of the National Park lies to the south, in the more complex area of Meirionnydd which can be thought of as a

Below: Snowdon's summit appears to dwarf that of Y Lliwedd here, although it is in fact less than 200m higher. Cloud formed in a temperature inversion is flowing between them

Opposite: Cader Idris from the east. This peak, Mynydd Pencoed, lies on the Minffordd path to the summit

triangle with Bala at its apex and Penrhyndeudraeth and Aberdyfi the two other points. Here the mountains and valleys are of different shapes and sizes to their larger cousins and they were created not only from volcanic ash but also from deposited gravel and mud. They are much more varied in character than their northern relatives. They are guarded by the southern sentinel of Snowdonia, the impressive mountain of Cader Idris. Cader Idris may mean the 'chair of Idris'. Idris was a giant who hurled stones and spat at Rita Gawr sitting on Snowdon: that's why we have so many lakes and rocks scattered throughout the land separating these old protagonists!

This then is the essence of Snowdonia – a huge variety of landscapes and habitats packed tightly together, close to the sea and imbued in mythology. You cannot escape the sea in Snowdonia – almost every mountain offers you glimpses of it. The great sweep of Tremadog Bay from Criccieth to Harlech can make the giants of the mountains pale into insignificance and under the sea is said to lie 'Cantref Gwaelod' – the mythical lost land of milk and honey. In Aberdyfi, if you are sensitive enough and the circumstances are right, you'll hear the bells of Cantref Gwaelod.

The rivers of Snowdonia flow from the mountains to the sea, and because of the shortness of their length they transform themselves from mountain torrent to placid, meandering rivers in a few miles. In the highlands, spectacular waterfalls are highlighted by their white streaks gashing the dark hills, while lower down the river courses equally spectacular cataracts attract visitors by the thousands. The classic example is Swallow Falls at Betws y Coed, incorrectly translated from the much more apposite Welsh name – Rhaeadr Ewennol – the foamy rapids.

And so the juxtaposition of water, soil and rock provide the ingredients for the habitats of Snowdonia. The peaks and ridges act like impervious roofs and the water runs off to form the streams and rivers while between them are the expanses of bogland where the water is retained. Here the acidic nature of the soil is a major factor in the formation of peat. If allowed to remain undisturbed for thousands of years, these peat grounds convert to blanket bogs as we see on the Migneint (which actually means a blanket bog) between Ffestiniog and Bala.

'The great sweep of Tremadog Bay …'

As the streams find their way down through ravines and gorges their moisture-laden sides harbour unassuming but valuable bryophytes. As the valleys widen, the rivers courses are embraced by woodlands and the sessile oaks which clad the valley flanks are a distinctive feature, as can be seen at Dyffryn Maentwrog (the Vale of Maentwrog) where Plas Tan y Bwlch, the Snowdonia National Park's Study Centre, is located.

In summer, the woodlands are populated by migrants such as the pied flycatchers, who join the permanent inhabitants and busy themselves in house-building and nannying. While Eryri may no longer be a home for eagles there are plenty of other birds of prey. The woodland birds fear the deadly sparrowhawk, while the buzzard circles above, preferring to prey on small mammals. The mountains are the base of the peregrine falcon and from berths further south a visitor of increasing frequency is the red kite.

And so life as in any mountain region is a mixture of beauty and harshness – a struggle for survival for animal and human alike. The cycle of life and death is a close companion in Snowdonia. Its inhabitants comprehend the necessity of death but also the inevitability of time. These are the facts of life in a fairly unyielding rural environment. As a locally-based poet described himself:

Wyf wanwyn o wanwynau fy nhylwyth
('I am the springtime of the springtimes of my people')
– but he also knows, in time, someone else –
A'r praidd i waered, rhag i'r pridd oeri
('will follow my footsteps in moving the flock to keep the soil warm').

Above: (top) Mosses and bryophytes; (below) Cymerau Gorge in the Vale of Ffestiniog, whose banks are clothed with native sessile oak woodland

Opposite: (top) Rocks laid bare by glaciation above Cwm Nantcol, showing characteristic striations; (below) Dyffryn burial chamber, a neolithic site dating back to the third or fourth millennium BC, in the village of Dyffryn Ardudwy

The Ice Ages were the great moulders of Snowdonia. It was the glaciers who found the weaker rocks amongst the solid volcanics, gouged out the cwms and the valleys and took with them much of the soil of the area as they ground their way to the sea. And while this legacy gives us the classic shape of Cwm Idwal and a home for Arctic-Alpines such as the Snowdon lily, it also dictated a destiny of predominant poverty for the people. Perhaps it is only now that we are beginning to turn that beauty into bread, and the designation of the Snowdonia National Park in 1951 was a major factor in that process.

Such matters would hardly have been a consideration to the original human colonisers. The record of continuous human occupation begins as the last glaciers shrunk and finally disappeared from their last mountain retreats some 10,000 to 12,000 years ago. These first human incursors would have been hunters who hardly made an impact on the natural environment. Everything changed as the economy transformed from hunting to farming during the Agricultural Revolution. The development of agriculture enabled Man to live a more settled life, and recent research has shown that the primeval woodlands began to be cleared in Britain around 3000BC.

It was Neolithic man who began the forest clearance that has continued ever since. The only evidence see today of those first colonisers are their burial chambers and a significant number are to be found on the coastal platform in Dyffryn Ardudwy between Harlech and Barmouth. Early travel would have been by sea and as the Neolithic imperceptibly merged into the Bronze Age more land became available and technology improved. It is now clear that Bronze Age man exploited the land more than we have considered hitherto and in Llandudno the Great Orme Copper Mines attest to his ingenuity.

Ingenuity was certainly the trait of the Celt. It was the use of iron that made the Celtic warriors unstoppable in Europe and their influence on Snowdonia and indeed Wales is immeasurable. With the Celtic incursion came the seeds of language and cultural identity that still play such an important part in the life of the area today. The debate about the nature of that 'incursion', when it happened and how, is a fierce one among archaeologists and historians. To most people, however, the Iron Age and the coming of the Celt mark the beginning of the Welsh people as we know them. The hill fort site at Bryn Castell, Llan Ffestiniog, excavated and consolidated by the Snowdonia National Park Authority, attests to the iron-working skills of the people of the last centuries before the birth of Christ.

Celtic culture is closely associated with the topography and some of the myths and legends hinge on the use of iron. Welsh myths as seen in the classic Welsh Medieval collection, *Y Mabinogion*, refer to specific areas and specific persons or gods. Lleu was a Celtic god who is identified in Nantlle (the vale of Lleu) or Dinas Dinlle (the Court of Lleu) but his life is closely linked to Bryn Castell and may indicate a great significance to that site. But in Snowdonia most of the hills and valleys, rivers and lakes have tales associated within them and each has a story to tell. Getting to that story is getting to the heart of Snowdonia but it is a mighty challenge. It requires great sensitivity to landscape and its interlinks with culture, a great deal of lateral thinking and possibly a sense of humour.

A sense of humour is not something that one associates very much with the Roman impact, rather a sense of order and authority. Roman occupation was characterised by a network of forts and roads centred on Segontium in present day Caernarfon, but they certainly brought prosperity with their trade and commerce.

Legend has it that Magnus Maximus claimed the western Roman Empire from his base at Segontium in

Above: Walkers on the summit of Carnedd Ugain, part of the Snowdon Horseshoe, early in the morning

Opposite: Llwybr Cam, which linked the town of Blaenau Ffestiniog with the Oakeley quarry above it

Pages 14–15: A perfect winter's day in the mountains: Crib Goch (right), the summit of Snowdon and Llyn Llydaw

Pages 18–19: Moel y Gest (in the centre of this image), near Porthmadog, is outside the Park, but is a real mountain in miniature. The view from its summit must be one of the most spectacular in the British Isles

383BC, but the woman behind the throne was Helen, a Celtic princess who put her name to the first trunk road system in Wales – Sarn Helen. On the departure of the Romans, again according to legend/history, the seeds of a Welsh governance was planted in the Roman purple.

For some 500 years the Welsh went through the agony of the creation of a state which reached its apogee with Llywelyn Fawr (Llywelyn the Great). He had strong connections with Dolwyddelan Castle, but was killed in 1282 by the relative newcomers, the Anglo-Normans. The Welsh state was not to be. The Norman castles, quite distinct from their Welsh counterparts, formed the noose around Snowdonia that throttled Welsh independence – Caernarfon, Conwy, Criccieth, Harlech and Beaumaris in Anglesey. Perhaps it's a sign of changing times that Caernarfon is now a tourist hot-spot and a venue for concerts and *son et lumière* displays.

Following the rebellion of Owain Glyndwr from 1400 to 1410, the area went into decline. The advent of Welsh-connected Henry VII to the throne of England prompted his son Henry VIII to pass the Act of Union in 1536 when Wales was incorporated into England and the Welsh language was banished. Fortuitously, his daughter Elizabeth I ordered the translation of the Bible into Welsh. The task, completed in 1588, was undertaken by a Snowdonia resident, Bishop William Morgan of Tŷ Mawr Wybrnant, near Penmachno, now the property of the National Trust. The Welsh language had become an issue!

Mention has been made of the Agricultural Revolution and its continuing impact but the next revolution, the Industrial Revolution, also made its mark in the

area. This was mainly through the development of the slate industry and its associated works and settlements. The slate quarrying areas of Bethesda, Nantlle, Ffestiniog, Llanberis and Corris have had an indelible effect on Snowdonia whether they are within its boundaries or not. Although the slate industry is still a major player in the area functions do change, as we have seen in the case of the castles. The former workshops of the Dinorwig Quarry in Llanberis now house the North Wales Slate Museum, and Llechwedd Quarry in Blaenau Ffestiniog is a major tourist attraction as well as being a working mine.

A wind-pruned oak tree on the banks of the Mawddach estuary

And Snowdonia is no stranger to tourism. Travellers have been coming into the area to marvel and the sights from the eighteenth century onwards. Thomas Pennant wrote his *Tours of Wales* in 1783 where he described his horrendous journey from Cwm Orthin, Ffestiniog to Cwm Croesor – a walk now enjoyed by many visitors to the National Park. William Wordsworth, so closely associated with the genesis of the National Parks movement, referred to his ascent of Snowdon in 'The Prelude' (1805). No doubt the Romantics led by Wordsworth were instrumental in raising people's awareness of the beauties of nature and the threats to them and laid the seeds of the National Park movement.

But, perhaps, as George Borrow said in his popular guide *Wild Wales*, published in 1853, the 'English only discovered Wales' in that period when mines and quarries opened up and were connected to the main markets by the railway network. This stimulated the period of mass tourism so feared by many Romantics of the nineteenth century. The Cambrian Railway connecting Birmingham to Pwllheli was opened in 1888 and coastal villages along the railway suddenly acquired a new status and, in many cases, a new name to accommodate the latest influx from the east. Barmouth (Abermaw) is a case in point and somehow the line still survives as well as the viaduct which still crosses the spectacular Mawddach Estuary.

Another surprising survivor is the Welsh language. Sixty-five per cent of the National Park's 26,000 inhabitants still have Welsh as their first language. Visitors notice the language because road signs and other notices

Welsh poppies

are bilingual, and they will also hear and listen to its sounds in all walks of life. Even if they do not understand the language they will appreciate the added dimension it brings to the richness of Snowdonia, and how much it is a part of that special understanding that underlie our National Parks – each one has its own secret.

And that reflects the great challenge to the Snowdonia National Park today. The second largest National Park in Britain, it holds some of the best natural treasures of the UK – features that the public 'own' through the enjoyment and appreciation they experience from them. In contrast, day-to-day life within and around those features is not as easy. Snowdonia, like the other National Parks, needs to show that beauty can and will mean bread, that the communities within them, both natural and human have to be viable and dynamic. They must retain their individual characteristics which hold the secret of their identity.

To get the best out of the area you should be prepared to work a little and be sensitive to so many nuances. As the world-famous poet who lives in Snowdonia, R. S. Thomas, says in *The Small Window*:

> *In Wales there are jewels*
> *To gather, but with the eye*
> *Only …*

But he also warns

> *Those who crowd*
> *A small window dirty it*
> *With their breathing, though sublime*
> *And inexhaustible the view.*

Hopefully, this guide may provide a number of windows on what makes Snowdonia so special and why it should be protected.

Llandecwyn church, in its prominent and solitary position high above the Dwyryd estuary, lies 2km from the village of the same name

1 The rocks beneath: geology and scenery

Below: In Cwm Caseg, a remote and untrodden valley in the northern Carneddau

Opposite: Glacial moraines (top of picture) in Cwm Tregalan, with the ruins and waste tips of Hafod y Llan quarry on the foreground

People are generally content to take the origins of scenery for granted. If they do try to explain it, they evoke volcanoes for the creation of mountains and earthquakes to account for gorges. Alternatively, many think that everything happened in the Ice Age and the mountains and valleys are all the result of the work of ice and glaciers.

In fact, those clearly over-simplistic views contain the kernels of the main forces of landscape creation. Many of the mountains of Snowdonia are the product of volcanic eruptions and the structure of the area has much to do with earth movement, and the effects of ice have been both dramatic and ubiquitous. What is missing from the above description is an acknowledgement of the differences in the nature of the raw material itself and time scale. The forces that have created the scenery of Snowdonia were felt throughout what is now the British Isles, but a major factor in what distinguishes one area from another is largely the character of the rocks, how hard or soft they may be – or what is termed their competence.

MOUNTAINS OF FUTURE AGES

In trying to explain the construction of the present scenery we are entering into time scales and magnitudes of forces beyond our imagination. A marvellous introduction is to be found in the Collins' New Naturalist volume on Snowdonia, published in 1949 – a must for any student of the area. In F. J. North's chapter on 'Mountains and Valleys', he reminds us that: 'The mountains of today are built of the debris of the mountains of the past and they owe the characters for which we admire them to the fact that they are disintegrating to provide raw materials for the mountains of future ages.'

North emphasises the role of 'imagination' based on sound knowledge to draw geological maps and writes the following astounding but correct observation: 'Having done this we realise, perhaps for the first time, that the magnificence of our area is due less to the rocks that remain than to those which have been worn away.'

Today we would interpret the history of rocks and scenery rather differently. But the tradition of investigation continues. Perhaps the technology evident in television natural history programmes does succeed in opening the doors to our understanding of the history of the earth. Still, it's a mighty leap from looking at wonderful graphics on TV to identifying those forces in the landscape around us. Another means of getting to grips with the forces of geology is to look at current volcanic areas and their activities and try to apply them to Snowdonia. But do we really have the 'imagination' of North or breadth of vision to visualise the apparent solidity of the Carneddau being the plastic, mobile terrain of volcanic Iceland?

This fact, coupled with the degree of the forces exerted on the rocks, are the predominant factors in building the foundations of the present topography. And, of course, it did not all happen at the same time.

The first dimension to appreciate is the time scale. It is now generally acknowledged that the Earth is over 4,600 million years old. The oldest rocks in Wales are about 600 million years old and it was at this time that life forms began to appear. So what we must grasp is that for 4,000 million years of the Earth's existence we know little of what went on. Normally, when we discuss geology, we refer to about only just over one tenth of that existence when there was life on Earth. Having said that, Wales and Snowdonia in particular contain evidence from most of that immense time period – and a lot can happen in 600 million years.

Rocks can be broadly divided into three types: *sedimentary*, *igneous* and *metamorphic*. Sedimentary rocks are those that are made up of deposited material; igneous are either solidified lava flows or ashes, the product of the eruptions of volcanoes; and metamorphic rocks are those that have been changed by the forces of movement or heat or both. All three types are to be found in Snowdonia and this fact, in itself, goes some way to explaining the variety within the area. Sedimentary rocks are generally more susceptible to the forces of erosion, while the igneous are more resistant, and the metamorphics are somewhere in between.

The three main geological ages that concern us are the Cambrian, Ordovician and Silurian. These are internationally acknowledged, of course, but it is worth noting that all three names have a Welsh connection – Cambria being an old name for Wales, and Ordovician and Silurian are derived from the names of Celtic tribes of north and mid Wales. This shows how Wales played its part in the development of the science of geology. It was in Snowdonia that a great dispute about the dating of rocks was resolved in the early nineteenth century, and it was here also that the effects of the Ice Ages in Britain were first acknowledged at the same time.

In addition to the ages of the rocks, another major factor has been the geological forces working on them. Thus, during the Silurian Age we have the mountain-building period called the Caledonian Orogeny (and, yes, this is when the mountains of Scotland largely came into being). The Earth's surface is made up of plates that 'float' on a more plastic interior, and from time to time these plates move and clash in response to currents emanating from the Earth's core. As they bump up against each other, the surface of the Earth at the point of contact is contorted into all kinds of shapes, and the movement causes volcanoes and earthquakes.

Southern Snowdonia is characterised in geological terms by the Harlech Dome. This is the area south of the Moelwyn Mountains to Cader Idris, and from the coast of Dyffryn Ardudwy to Bala. The predominant rock types are sedimentary and belong to the Cambrian Age and the term 'dome' refers to the time when the older Cambrian 'plate' was being 'nudged' by the younger Ordovician rocks to the north and the even younger Silurian rocks to the south, during the Caledonian Orogeny. The middle part of the Harlech Dome is now largely subdued as the sedimentary rocks have been eroded, as seen on the A470 road from Dolgellau to Trawsfynydd or from Bala to Trawsfynydd (A4212).

But emerging out of the softer landscape are the piles of ashes from volcanic eruptions compressed into rocks of the Ordovician Age that have withstood those forces to form peaks such as Rhobell Fawr and Rhobell Fach, Arenig Fawr and Arenig Fach; Moel Offrwm above Dolgellau, and Y Garnedd above Ganllwyd. The range that rises between the coastline and the interior – the Rhinogydd; Rhinog Fawr and Fach in the middle; Diffwys and Y Llethr to their south; Moel Penolau and Moel Ysgyfarnogod to their north – are an exception. These are sedimentary gravels of the Cambrian Age revealed by their blocky structure which make for the most difficult wild country walking in Snowdonia.

Above: (top) Rugged hill country and poor agricultural land east of Harlech, with Rhinog Fawr on the skyline; (below) landscape of rock and ice on the summit of Glyder Fawr, with Glyder Fach in the background

Opposite: Sheepfold in the Anafon valley, one of several similar in the northern foothills of the Carneddau

Left: Snowdon summit from Crib y Ddysgl
Above: Quartz-veined rock above the Aberglaslyn Pass

The most spectacular walking area, arguably, is to the north of the Moelwynion – the heart of Eryri itself. This is where the peaks and ridges attest mightily to Earth's unlimited creative forces. The Snowdon Horseshoe is the central core – Yr Aran, Lliwedd, Gallt y Wenallt, Yr Wyddfa, Crib y Ddysgl and Crib Goch. Referring to North again, we should bear two facts in mind regarding the summit of Snowdon, Yr Wyddfa. The first is that the present summit is the lowest point of a geological downfold (syncline) and that amazingly, seashore fossils can be found high on the mountain. To the north-west are Glyder Fawr and Glyder Fach and the unmistakable Tryfan. These again are predominantly ashes with one single uninterrupted layer in Cwm Idwal being about 800ft (260m) deep. What size volcano would deposit 260 metres of ash? And, as in Iceland, it did rise straight out of sea.

To the north, the Ordovician rocks change to the Cambrian, and though the mountains are as high they do not express the same tortuous history as their younger neighbours. Carnedd Llywelyn and Carnedd Dafydd, Foel Grach and Moel Fras have a more mature look somehow, and even Pen yr Ole Wen has a softer aspect. But we must not be deceived by their more rounded summits; they also have their precipitous slopes as anybody who knows

Overleaf: The distinctive outline of Tryfan, with a small plantation of Scots pine in the foreground

Ysgolion Duon will tell you. North of Cwm Idwal, on the western side of Nant Ffrancon, the boundary between the rock ages is crossed imperceptibly on the route from Y Garn to Moel Perfedd and Moel Elidir. It seems as if Moel Elidir has had the attention of a mythological dentist as two huge cavities are seen on both side of the ridge. These are the slate quarries of Penrhyn in Bethesda and Dinorwig in Llanberis which exploited Cambrian slate. But in the mountains of the Moelwyn it was the Ordovician slate that was mined, and on the southern edge of the boundary of the National Park in the Corris area are quarries of Silurian slate.

Whatever the colour of rocks (and slates) the primacy of greyness is an important characteristic. Snowdonia rocks tend to be different shades of grey

Above: The massive tips of Dinorwig quarry

Right: The market town of Dolgellau, with its distinctive stone architecture

and this is because of the high content of silica. Internally, the rocks are multi-coloured, but as they weather, the silica on the surface transforms into grey – the darker the grey, the higher the silica content. Silica in its concentrated form is the main constituent mineral of quartz. Under intense pressure during the mountain-building periods, silica would flow in solution before crystallising into veins and those white quartz veins are a signal for mineralisation – another by-product of the mountain building forces. During the time when slate was being formed, other minerals in company with silica coursed in veins through the plastic rock and then, as the pressure and temperature eased, they also crystallised out into their distinctive identities.

Snowdonia has long been known for its mineral wealth – mainly copper, lead/zinc and gold. Just outside the northernmost point of the Park lies Llandudno and on the Great Orme are substantial workings dating to the Bronze Age. Near Llyn Llydaw on Snowdon a canoe of the same period has been discovered.

Between the summit itself and Llyn Glaslyn, copper was mined from the eighteenth century to the beginning of the twentieth. The shell of the processing plant

THE SLATE FACTOR

Slate more than any other rock exemplifies the geological history of Snowdonia. It is a metamorphic rock that started as a sedimentary rock deposited under marine conditions and then, over a period of millions of years, had its nature changed under heat and pressure. Originally deposited as a mudstone made up of flaky clay minerals, these minerals were compressed to line up parallel to each other to create what we call 'shales'. In the mountain-building period the stratified layers in the shales were then subject to further pressure and heat. The heat was so intense that the clay minerals were broken up and re-constituted as new minerals of feldspar and mica, but the pressure they were under forced them to realign along a totally new plane. This new plane is called the 'plane of cleavage' and it is along this that the slate easily splits to give it its economic value as a roofing material.

The Cambrian slates of the north are multi-coloured, hard but brittle; the Ordovician slates are predominantly blue grey and more supple while the Silurian are a lighter grey and poorer quality. While the huge forces of geology created the slate industry, the industry itself was the cause of the major economic and social forces that has made Snowdonia what it is today in human terms. The interpretation of this influential industry is well covered through the North Wales Slate Museum at Llanberis and the Llechwedd Slate Caverns at Blaenau Ffestiniog, a working mine.

Above: There was a plan to re-open
the disused Rhosydd slate quarry,
between Croesor and Blaenau
Ffestiniog, in the 1990s. Even though
permission was granted, development
is unlikely

Opposite: (top) Crib Goch – the
red ridge – from the summit of
Snowdon; (below) Nant Francon –
a classic glacial trough

of the Britannia Works of 1904 has been consolidated by the Snowdonia National Park Authority. If you do take the Miners' Track to the summit, just consider what it would have been like to climb that slope with a sack of copper ore on your back, which is what the miners of the eighteenth century had to do. A little south in Cwm Bychan (Nanmor), the National Trust has consolidated remains of copper workings including the stanchions for an aerial ropeway dating from about 1916. In the nineteenth century, Beddgelert was a village of miners as well as farm workers, and just outside the village the former copper mine of Sygun is now, like the village itself, a tourist attraction.

Lead and zinc are found in the north-east of the Park, mainly in the Gwydir Forest. Here, Forestry Enterprise working with the National Park Authority has consolidated the remains of some of the mines, such as Llanrwst and Hafna, and the Miners Bridge near Betws y Coed was indeed a miners' path at one time. Betws y Coed, like Beddgelert, was originally a mining settlement, but the coming of the railway stimulated the already established tourist industry and the village was transformed.

Gold was a much later discovery, but in the 1840s, 1860s and 1890s led to significant 'gold rushes' in Dyffryn Mawddach. Dolgellau was a boom town at the turn of the century, when some 500 men were employed in the gold (and copper) mines of the district. In 1898, A. J. Bradley in his *Highways and Byways of North Wales* described the Mawddach thus, when the Glasdir Mine was pounding away at its maximum capacity: '... for the once bright Mawddach now goes leaping down its winding glen from Ty'n ŷ Groes to Cymmer, a torrent of thick milk.'

And, of course, the demands of mining are often at odds with the need to protect the qualities of the National Park. Mining and quarrying are, by their very

CWM OF ALL CWMS

The steep back wall with the Idwal Slabs have helped many to gain their climbing skills, but the feature that stands out in Cwm Idwal is Twll Du (Devil's Kitchen). Here the fold of the rock has been rent asunder by the power of the ice tearing its way from the back wall before excavating the floor of the hollow and scraping over the lip to continue its work in the main valley of Nant Ffrancon below. The bare rocks are smooth but scarred and their polished surfaces seem to indicate the direction of the ice. But below Twll Du the tumble of the boulder scree attests to unfinished business at the end of the last Ice Age. Extraction was continuing but transportation was not – the retreating glacier could not carry the detritus away. Below the scree are linear mounds of clay and stones – moraines that accumulated at the tip of the tongue of the turbid ice. Strange to think that the great Darwin himself on his first visit to Cwm Idwal failed to detect the signs of glacial activity. It took a man from Switzerland, Louis Aggazziz, to see the links between the Alps and Snowdonia, but Darwin being the man he was acknowledged Aggazziz's work and changed his mind.

Llyn Idwal set within the formidable cliffs of its cwm is a classic example of the action of ice on the landscape; Glyder Fawr behind left

The 'green carpet' of Dyffryn Conwy and the village of Llanrwst

nature, destructive and cannot but leave significant evidence of activity in the landscape. National Park legislation now demands that mining should not take place in National Parks unless no alternative is available and it is in the public interest to allow it. This can clearly cause conflict in the area, between the need for employment and the need for protection of amenity. This was the case with the Rhosydd Slate Quarry high on the Moelwyn Mountain in the 1990s. Walk from Moelwyn Mawr to Cnicht past the cavities of the nineteenth-century operation and the mills and the barracks, and just imagine a modern-day quarrying operation at over 1000ft (330m) up in Bwlch Rhosydd. It would have been devastating. But then look down at Blaenau Ffestiniog with its closed shops and poverty, high unemployment and consider the plight of the young people there. Yes, geology and topography are not always happy partners of economy but that is a challenge for the Snowdonia National Park Authority and other agencies operating in the area today.

But perhaps the most destructive force evident throughout Snowdonia is in fact natural, and that is the work of the ice. The great screes of Nant Peris are the waste tips of the processes of glacial and ice erosion as is the detritus that clutters the mountain tops throughout the area. But, in a similar way to the slate industry, the Ice Ages and their aftermath can be creative in some places and destructive in others. Without doubt, its legacy is part of the heritage of Snowdonia.

That legacy is nowhere more evident than in the narrow ridges, the cwms and glacial troughs that are such essential characteristics. Crib Goch (the red ridge) is there because the glacial flow found hollows on both sides of the ridge and then deepened and steepened them so that the thin apex now plunges towards Llyn Glaslyn on one side and into the dark and mysterious Cwm Glas on the other.

On the Watkin Path up Snowdon you can look down on Cwm Tregalan (the place of woe) with huge mounds at the base of the cliff. While some say that these are glacial moraines, others will tell you that the 'woe' in the name comes about because these are the burial mounds of the cream of King Arthur's army, cut down by the enemy as they shot their arrows of Bwlch y Saethau (the pass of arrows). And, of course, not far away, Arthur and his cohorts are resting in a cave on Lliwedd, waiting for the call.

There are cwms everywhere and below these excavated hollows in the mountain sides are the main glacial troughs of Snowdonia, characterised by the steep sides and relatively wide and flat floors. Down from Cwm Idwal is Nant Ffrancon, and Nant Peris lies between Glyder Fach and Snowdon, while south of Snowdon is Nant Gwynant. The most spectacular and illustrative cwm is Cwm Croesor as seen from the view at the head of the Rhosydd Quarry Incline down to the sea.

We must not forget that the river valleys are much wider than they ought to be because of the Ice Age. The wide Dyffryn Conwy is not only the result of the erosion of the Afon Conwy but of its enlargement by a glacier and the same can be said of the spectacular Dyffryn Mawddach. Equally dramatic is the landscape of the Dyfi Valley. Here the softer Silurian foundation has resulted in rounder contours as we see in Cwm Cywarch or the strikingly beautiful and beautifully named Llaethnant Dyfi – the source of the Dyfi at the southern foot of Aran Fawddwy. All were formed by the same forces, but different raw materials.

What we must also keep in mind is that what we see is a combination of so many different factors. This is seen most spectacularly along the geological formation known as the Bala-Chester Fault. This is the fault line that defines the

Autumn colours in the Mawddach estuary

The mouth of the Mawddach near Barmouth, with the sandspit, Ro Wen, formed by the debris from the erosion of the cliffs further south

Opposite: Llyn Mwyngil at Tal y Llyn

boundary between the Cambrian/Ordovician complex from the periphery of the southern Silurian. It goes from Tywyn north-east through Talyllyn, south of the Aran Fawddwy/Benllyn Ridge through Bala and then the Dee follows it to Chester. Along this fault the inherent geological weakness has been exploited by the glacial forces to create the spectacular valleys of Talyllyn with its lake, Llyn Mwyngil and on to Llyn Tegid and the dramatic Dee Valley. This major geological fault follows a south-west to north-east trend which can be seen in the land from Snowdonia, through the Lake District to Scotland.

Then there is the coastline. The Snowdonia coast is predominantly what is called an emergent coastline. This means that it's one where the deposition of material is the major factor rather then erosion. Thus we have the build-up of the sand dunes, best seen at Harlech. Another feature is the sandspit such as the one created at the mouth of the Mawddach, where the holiday village of Fairbourne has been built on the 'new' ground built up from deposits of the erosion of the cliffs further south.

When we look at the physical aspect of Snowdonia, perhaps we should regard them in their totality and appreciate that human forces combine with natural forces to produce the full picture. As you walk the Watkin Path on Snowdon you'll see the mounds of Cwm Tregalan and the slate tips of the Hafod y Llan Quarry. Together they provide the distinctive landscape of that place – the hand of nature and the human hand combining to create the whole.

Throughout Snowdonia, the hand of humanity is there in stronger or lighter touches and forms part of the dynamic. Nothing stands still, and as we protect the essential qualities of our National Park we should always bear in mind that it is an organic entity and the real challenge is the challenge of change – and its management.

2 Climate, vegetation and wildlife

From the sea to the mountains ('o'r môr i ben y mynydd' in Welsh) is the essential theme of Snowdonia, and the variety implicit in that statement is highlighted in this chapter. And never more so than in the main driving force of climate and vegetation – rain.

'Glaw, fe ddaw fel y mynn' (Rain comes as it will) says a Snowdonia-born national poet, and surely this is right. But in the case of rainfall, as with so many other characteristics of the region, it's not only its abundance that is noticeable but its variety. The summit of Snowdon may have some 200in (5,080mm) of rain a year but the coastline, only some 12 miles away only has about 30in (760mm), and in between we find a range of gradation on the slopes, cwms and valleys.

With the rain come clouds and mists. How often does the traveller from Maentwrog to Blaenau Ffestiniog enter the cloud just below the town and how often, from the opposite direction, do travellers from Dolwyddelan, as they cross the highest point of Bwlch Gorddinan (Crimea Pass), descend into the cloud embraced by the hollow between the Moelwynion and Manod? How often have I trudged along the Nantlle Ridge clasped in mist only for it unexpectedly to loosen its grasp, and been rewarded with tremendous vistas opening up over Dyffryn Nantlle or Cwm Pennant or onto Snowdon itself?

Below: Rainclouds over the Mawddach estuary

Opposite: Rhaeadr Fawr, Abergwyngregyn – commonly known as Aber Falls – on the northern edge of the Carneddau

MIGNEINT – A NATURAL MOSAIC

The source of the word 'Migneint' is 'mign,' which literally means a blanket bog, and on Migneint the discerning observer can discover a wonderful mosaic of the habitats of the uplands. On the drier areas, heather and bilberry are seen accompanied by a variety of lichens, while the wetter areas are the home of the mosses, especially the sphagnums. The sphagnum areas contain insectivorous plants and prominent among them are the rosettes of the sundews with their hairy, paddle-shaped leaves. Flies should beware – and humans too. Where the sphagnum is its brightest lie the danger areas for walkers, because beneath that lurid surface lies the greatest depth of water. My personal experience of being waste-deep in stinking, peaty water was a lesson well-learned.

It is the peat, of course, that underlies the moor. Peat develops when soil conditions of acidity and wetness prevent the bacterial action of decay in plants and on the Migneint, the depth of peat is considerable. The peat supports a range of grasses, sedges and rushes with the wispy cotton-grass being a key species (it is known as plu gweunydd in Welsh meaning 'moorland feathers').

Thus Migneint and other moorland areas are a wonderful illustration of the attractions of the micro and macro scales. Look in detail and you will be fascinated by the range of plants, but step back and admire the sweep of the moor and its range of colours especially towards the end of the summer and in autumn.

Thus it is not rain that is the crucial factor but precipitation – precipitation in the form of drops of rain, droplets of mist, water vapour or dew and, of course, snow in its various forms. So much of what we see clothing our hills and valleys is the product of the interaction between precipitation and the raw material of rock and soil.

In terms of the impact of vegetation, it is not so much the mountains that are the most striking but the expanses of blanket bog, mire bogs and moors that stretch between them, and this is where the interaction between water and earth is so crucial. A dramatic approach to Snowdonia is along the A543 from Denbigh across the Denbigh Moors and Mynydd Hiraethog. This vast emptiness of heather and bog is an essential corollary to the sharp peaks of Eryri that protrude beyond it and reminds us that it is not only the landscape and habitats within the boundaries of the Park that are important, but the areas on its borders as well. Within the Park, in a triangle between Bala, Betws y Coed and Trawsfynydd, lies the largest expanse of blanket bog in Wales – Migneint.

Among those who appreciate the boglands are the birds of the moor, especially the birds of prey – they need the space but it's in the detail they'll pursue their prey. The kestrel is quite common and an occasional merlin may be seen, but it's the peregrine falcon ('yr hebog', in Welsh) who is the master killer of the sky in upland Snowdonia. Some guide books maintain that Moel Hebog, above Beddgelert, is named after this acrobatic sky-diver but, as it so often the case 'Hebog' is a corruption and 'Ehedog' is more correct, meaning 'the 'suspended' mountain'. We should not forget another acrobat of the skies – the chough. From nests in slate quarries, the red-beaked and legged chough twist, turns and plummets before soaring and squealing haughtily away into the distance.

The peregrines and the choughs take to the rocks to nest, as does another master of the sky – the raven. The croak of the raven is the cry of the all-seeing, all-knowing bird which has its place in Welsh mythology as it does in so many others throughout the world. It is a cry that can haunt the rock climber spread-eagled on a bare face.

Increasingly these days, you may be lucky to see the huge wing-span and the forked tail of the graceful red kite. The red kite is a bird of prey associated with

mid-Wales but successful re-establishment programmes means that these magnificent predators continue to expand their territory, and can now be seen around in Cwm Mawddwy and Cader Idris and even further north.

Perhaps it is the rock climber who may have the best opportunities to appreciate the special plants of the mountains of Snowdonia, the Arctic-Alpines. Hopefully the climber of today will be more aware than his predecessors of how precarious is the existence of these rare plants. How do Arctic-Alpine plants survive in Snowdonia? Are they survivors of plants that clung on the bare rocks protruding out of the glacier or are they the remnants of the rapid recolonisation that occurred as the Ice Age ended and have survived because other plants have not been able to succeed them? The answer is unclear, but either way their existence today depends on close observation and careful conservation management by statutory authorities such as the National Park and the Countryside Council for Wales, as well as non-governmental organisations such as the Wildlife Trusts and the RSPB. Ultimately, however, the efforts of all these agencies could be put in jeopardy without the understanding and co-operation of the ordinary visitor to the Park, as well as local residents.

In spring as the plants begin their re-awakening, the mountains witness new indicators of life with the return of the early migrants. One of the first is the flash of white from the tail of the wheatear, which betrays its more apposite pre-Victorian title of 'white arse' (the Welsh have retained the name 'tinwen'). Another welcome spring arrival is the ring ouzel whose white band is more respectably placed under its neck.

The natural history of Snowdonia is an ever-changing cyclical affair. In the winter the mountains and moorlands are stark and forbidding with, it seems, only the raven keeping an account of the occasional visitor. Come the spring, however and the bustle begins. In no time at all the uplands are transformed as the bowed heads of the purple moor grass become proud again and the sheep arrive to nibble at the young shoots. The larks begin to sing as they are joined by their friends from across the sea, and the walkers and tourists arrive in ever greater numbers.

But this transformation is even more noticeable in the valleys. The sides of the valleys are clothed in trees and no other habitat seems to fanfare the seasons to

Left: The 'hanging gardens' in Cwm Idwal, with early purple orchid, herb robert and globeflower

THE SNOWDON LILY

Undoubtedly the emblem of the Arctic-Alpines in Snowdonia is the Snowdon lily, Lloydia serotina, named after its discoverer, Edward Lluyd, reputedly the greatest European naturalist of the seventeenth century. It is an attractive plant when it

flowers briefly in June – with white flowers and grass-like leaves. However it has suffered over the years from avid collectors and now is confined to a few sites deep in the mountains.

A traditional home of the Snowdon lily is Cwm Idwal, but there are a lot more plants that can be enjoyed without searching for the rarest. A walk through the screes below Twll Du (Devil's Kitchen) will reveal other specialities such as the starry and mossy saxifrages and moss campion. Above the screes, near Twll Du are the 'hanging gardens' – ledges wetted by the leaching from the volcanic rocks. Here more than thirty species of flowering plants and ferns can be identified – a reminder of how important the raw material, ie the rock, is in producing the end result in terms of ecology. The basic volcanics are lime-rich and thus provide the nutrients for the plants to flourish, and their relative inaccessibility protects them from intruders.

The beautiful vale of Ffestiniog with Moelwyn Bach rising beyond it

quite the same degree as the sessile woodlands of the area. The trees have been bare and subdued in winter, but as soon as the buds begin to emerge and the young crooks of the spring bracken thrust their way through the battered brown layer of the old growth, the pace of life changes.

One presager of summer is the cuckoo and the first is heard in about mid-April. In my home valley of Cwm Croesor, the cuckoo regularly starts its two-note call about 20 April and within a few days, the altogether too-regular duo-tone seems to dominate life. As summer arrives the parent cuckoo returns overseas and the young cuckoos take full advantage of their foster-parents before later in the year embarking on their long journey south. This particularly miraculous cycle of migration caused the master naturalist, William Condry, to say in his 1966 guide to the National Park: '... once independent, the young cuckoos do not linger in the hills. Urged by instincts of which we understand nothing, guided by means about which we can only make guesses, they depart, each young bird alone, on a three thousand mile journey south.'

Cwm Croesor will greet the more mature birds next spring, and the cycle will be repeated as the regeneration occurs – a fact of life in Snowdonia from time immemorial.

On the other hand there is the resident bird population. In the woodlands we find the tits and their allies. Blue tits, great tits and coal tits scurry around in the brambles and on the tree trunks, the nuthatch patters up and down while its cousin the treecreeper scales the trunks in an upward direction only. Thrushes and blackbirds dash around while, above, the buzzard with its beady stare waits his chances with the smaller mammals of the woodland floor.

In many woodlands, all this is given a greater sense of urgency with the appearance of the pied flycatchers which, though common in Snowdonia, are not as numerous in other parts of the UK. CCW study these summer visitors in detail, especially in the National Nature Reserves at Dyffryn Maentwrog and Coedydd Aber, near Bangor, where they have erected nest boxes to facilitate their research.

Through Coedydd Aber flows the river, Afon Llafar, at 8 miles long, the shortest river in Wales. It starts on the lower slopes of the Carneddau, hurtles 500ft (152m) down Aber Falls, gurgles its way through the oak/alder woodland and enters the Menai Straits at Abergwyngregin (the mouth of the river with the white shells). The sharp descent of the rivers in Snowdonia provides numerous examples of gorges, waterfalls and cataracts where, once again, the interplay between water and rock and soil is so crucial.

Mention has already has been made of Rhaeadr Ewennol (Swallow Falls) and the fact that the origin of the name is, in fact, 'foamy rapids'. You have to pay to go and see the foamy rapids of Swallow Falls but there are countless others in Snowdonia that you can see for free. To the north of Swallow Falls are the cataracts of Pont Cyfyng, Capel Curig, and to the south, the Afon Lledr provides a number of examples where people can watch the salmon jumping the rapids. On the last falls of the Afon Conwy before it welcomes the Lledr near Pont yr Afanc (Beaver Bridge), Dŵr Cymru/Welsh Water have built a fish pass in the form of a tunnel as a contribution to maintaining the quality of the river. In these places and in many other hidden ravines, the humidity from rain, river and rapids create conditions for water-loving plants such as mosses and liverworts. In southern Snowdonia, communities of ferns such as the bladder fern and hard shield fern are found with a variety of the worts, including the spleenwort. The Torrent Walk

A carpet of bluebells amongst alder woodland in the Aber National Nature Reserve

*Opposite: The Machno Gorge just
above the Conwy Falls*

*Left: Boulders in the Afon Eden, in
Coed-y-Brenin north of Dolgellau*

near Dolgellau and the Dolgoch Falls near Tal y Llyn provide easy walks to observe these habitats and species.

The Llugwy, Machno/Conwy and Lledr rivers join together to nourish the queen of rivers of northern Snowdonia – Afon Conwy. Dyffryn Conwy from Glan Conwy near the coast, south to Betws y Coed, acts like a long, lush, green-carpeted entrance foyer into the core of the mountains.

Afon Wen, Eden, Wnion, Mawddach together create the Mawddach itself which meanders down the most spectacular valley in Snowdonia from Dolgellau to Barmouth below the majestic Cader Idris – Dyffryn Mawddach.

Further south, the Dyffryn Dysynni is broader and greener. In fact, the lower reaches of the estuary are called 'Broadwater', but inland from here where the sea used to reach is Craig Aderyn (Bird Rock), the only inland nesting place of cormorants. Right at the southern edge of the National Park, the mouth of the Dyfi is almost lost in the broad expanse of Borth stretching miles down to Ynyslas on the way to Aberystwyth. The estuaries of all these rivers teem with birdlife throughout the year. In the winter, migrating birds stop by to stock up before moving on, and waders can be seen nodding their beaks into the mud in search for food. These estuaries are of much more importance than to their immediate localities because they are providers of winter food for birds from all over the colder parts of the northern hemisphere. At the sea edge, oystercatchers catch the shellfish and in the wet mud you can always see redshanks, dunlin, grey and golden plover, sandpipers and curlews.

Arguably it is from Dyffryn Ardudwy near Harlech to the foot of Criccieth Castle rock, that the coast is at its best in terms of landscape and habitats. The view of Tremadog Bay from Llanfair is breathtaking. In fact, the National Trust has acquired some land at what is called 'Surprise View' to ensure that we can always enjoy this vista. Behind the great sweep of Harlech Beach are the sand dunes that are well worth a visit, but a good part of them are a Nature Reserve which require a permit from the Countryside Council for Wales. The dunes themselves are kept together by the ubiquitous marram grass whose roots go deep into the sand. Within the dunes are found a number of orchids and creeping willow, and on the

*Overleaf: The beautiful low-lying
valley of the Dysynni. Craig yr
Aderyn (above centre) is still the
nesting place of cormorants, which
are normally coastal*

slopes lady's bedstraw takes advantage of the lime-rich shelly sands. The dunes are, of course, constantly changing, but in many places that process has been accelerated to the point of destruction by the effects of people. The CCW has invested a great deal in sand stabilisation to give the habitat a chance so, please, treat the sand dunes with respect – wherever you may be.

Another dramatic change occurred in this area following the erection of the Cob, an embankment across the wide estuary of the Afon Glaslyn, in 1812. This was the work of William Alexander Maddocks who transformed Traeth Mawr from a tract of shifting sands and tidal water into fields. There was a great outcry at the time from some quarters about the loss of a habitats and views. It is interesting to note that the migratory whooper swans seem not to have fully realised the change (like the cormorants on Craig Aderyn), because they continue to return to their old haunts to graze the fields – much to the chagrin of the farmers. But all is not lost. The view of the Snowdon Massif from the Cob is special and the fact that the Central Electricity Generating Board was persuaded to underground its cables owes a great deal to the amenity protectionists of the early 1950s, particularly CPRW (Campaign for the Protection of Rural Wales). Also near the southern end of the Cob is the Glaslyn Nature Reserve – an area of wetland with a fascination all to itself in terms of plants and habitats.

But it is the gulls you will see and hear everywhere. Particularly noisy and profuse is the herring gull, but not far behind is the small black-headed gull. They will tuck at your sandwiches on the summit of Snowdon and they live quite happily, and noisily, on

The superb sandy beach at Harlech

YR AFANC

The otter's larger cousin, the beaver – yr afanc – was a common species many years ago, as medieval accounts and poetry show and many place names also attest. Near Betws y Coed, we have Pont yr Afanc and Llyn yr Afanc but we must be careful – 'afanc' in Welsh folklore could mean many things including a river monster. In this case, many, many years ago, the 'afanc' at the confluence of the Conwy and Lledr was causing mayhem in the area. A beautiful maiden enticed it out of its pool and it was chained. Two oxen then dragged the afanc up Dyffryn Lledr to Dolwyddelan and over Bwlch Rhiw'r Ychen (the pass of the slope of the oxen), where one ox lost one of its eyes, in a place still called Gwaun Llygad Ych (the moor of the ox's eye). Here a lake formed called Pwll Llygad Ych – the lake of the ox's eye. No water enters this lake and no water leaves it, but it is always the same depth. Eventually the oxen struggled up to Llyn Cwm Ffynnon Las (the lake in the cwm of the green well) where the afanc, far enough from habitation, was consigned. Many strange sights and many inexplicable disappearances have occurred here since. Today we know the lake as Llyn Glaslyn, and we pass by it on the Miners' Track up Snowdon – so keep a wary eye on the water. You can still trace the last journey of the afanc of Betws y Coed on a modern map.

Opposite: (top) Cymerau Gorge in the Vale of Ffestiniog – habitat of the dipper and grey wagtail. The gorge is a National Nature Reserve with restricted access; (below) The youthful river Dyfi

inland lakes such as Llyn yr Adar near Cnicht, and Llyn Elsi above Betws y Coed. These gregarious birds truly represent the theme of Snowdonia: from the sea to the top of the mountain.

And in that range of habitats the mammals busy themselves in the spring and summer but most will stay closer to home in winter. The stoat changes its coat to a more suitable white one for the cold months, but its smaller cousin, the weasel, will bear out the winter in the same guise as will the rarer polecat and pine marten. These animals are rarely seen by visitors to Snowdonia as they are few in numbers and wary of human presence.

Visitors are more likely to see are foxes and badgers. Foxes range all over Snowdonia and some have been seen on the higher slopes of Snowdon itself. Over the winter and early spring, farmers and others regularly hunt foxes in Snowdonia and use dogs to flush out the animal, which is then shot. There is no doubt that foxes do cause losses to the mountain farm and as long as there are plenty of places such as forest plantations for them to hide, they will continue to flourish and will need controlling. Badgers are more restricted in their range and do not wander far from their setts, which are now protected like the animal itself. Some will argue that badgers are also pests as far the farming stock is concerned, but a direct link between diseases in cows and badgers has not been proven. It seems at present that some control is exerted by the car as badgers, unwittingly perhaps, take to the road. Needless to say, the killing of any animal on the road is cruel and pointless and is another very good reason why driving in the National Park should be done with care.

The real hubbub of natural life lies along the rivers of the National Park. One of the most attractive birds in Snowdonia is the dipper. This small but neat bird patrols a length of river by flying swiftly just above the surface, then perches on a rock before dipping into the clear water to feed along the bed of the river – a fascinating sight. On the banks or patrolling the river you may be lucky enough to see the blue flash of the kingfisher. And in some places in the summer you will be graced by the presence of dragonflies, as you await your chance to see the river birds.

You may be lucky enough (but it would be a long wait normally) to see the shyest of the river animals – the otter (dyfrgi, in Welsh). After careful management of rivers, these animals now coming back to the rivers, but do not expect anyone to tell where you can find them – there's a long way to go yet before they are safe.

The influence of Man is inescapable. We cannot talk of the natural without taking account of human activities and the tale of the beaver/afanc shows how intimate was the relationship between our ancestors and the world around them. Today, much more of the land is under some form of management so that, in terms of the fauna of Snowdonia, the only animals you are guaranteed to see are sheep and cattle, but these are not wild. What you may also see is an animal that was once domesticated but has reverted to the wild – the feral goat. Before the dominance of sheep, goats were as numerous if not more so, but now in their semi-wild state they can still be seen on the rocks of the Rhinogydd mountains or on the Carneddau. When seen from afar, they look like majestic animals with their curved horns and straggling beards and coats, but make sure you are not downwind of them!

The purposes of the National Parks were modified in 1995 to include the protection and enhancement of wildlife and, while the Parks have always been about the care and protection of the environment generally, it must be for the good that there is now a specific reference to wildlife protection in their aims.

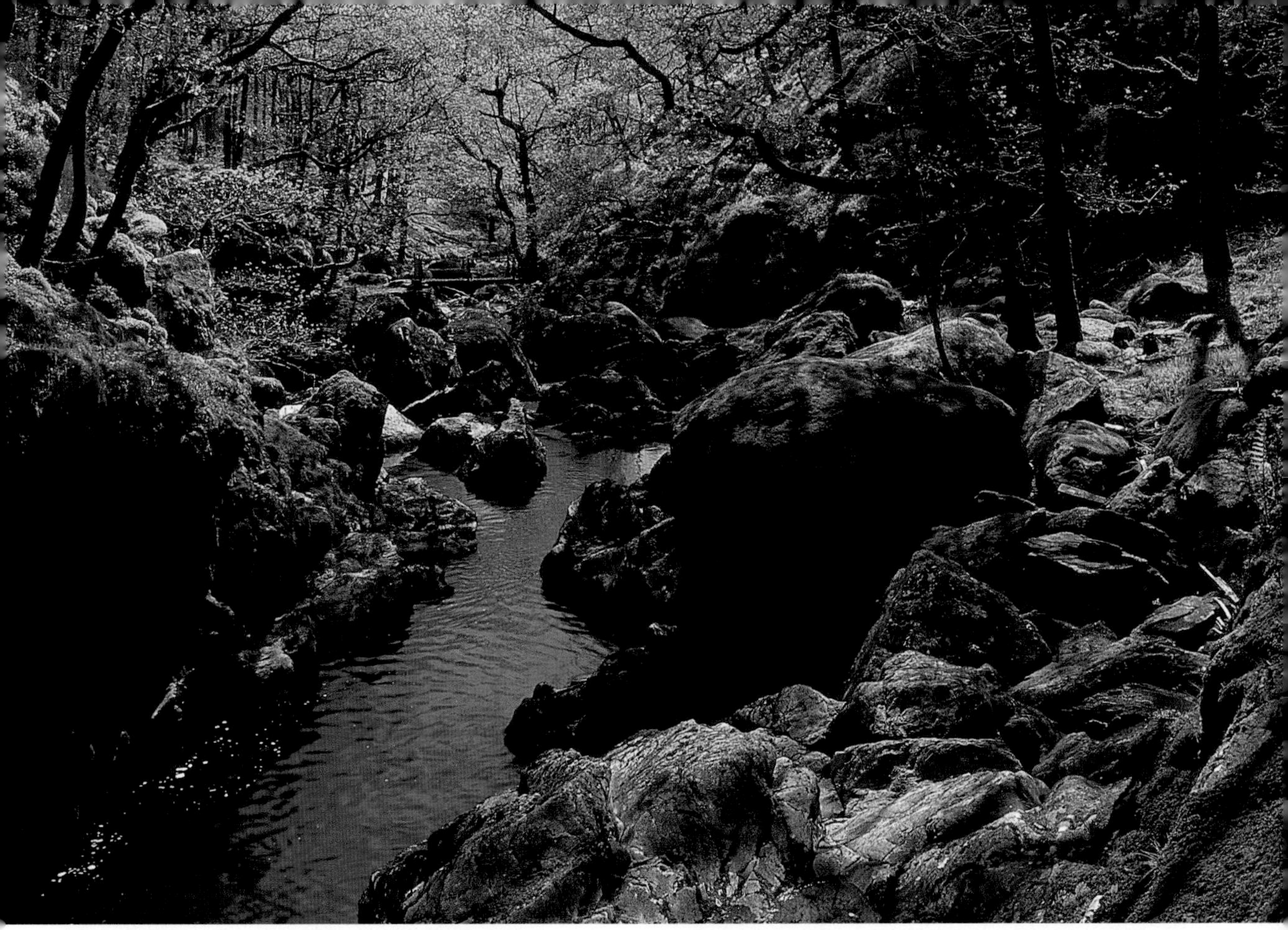

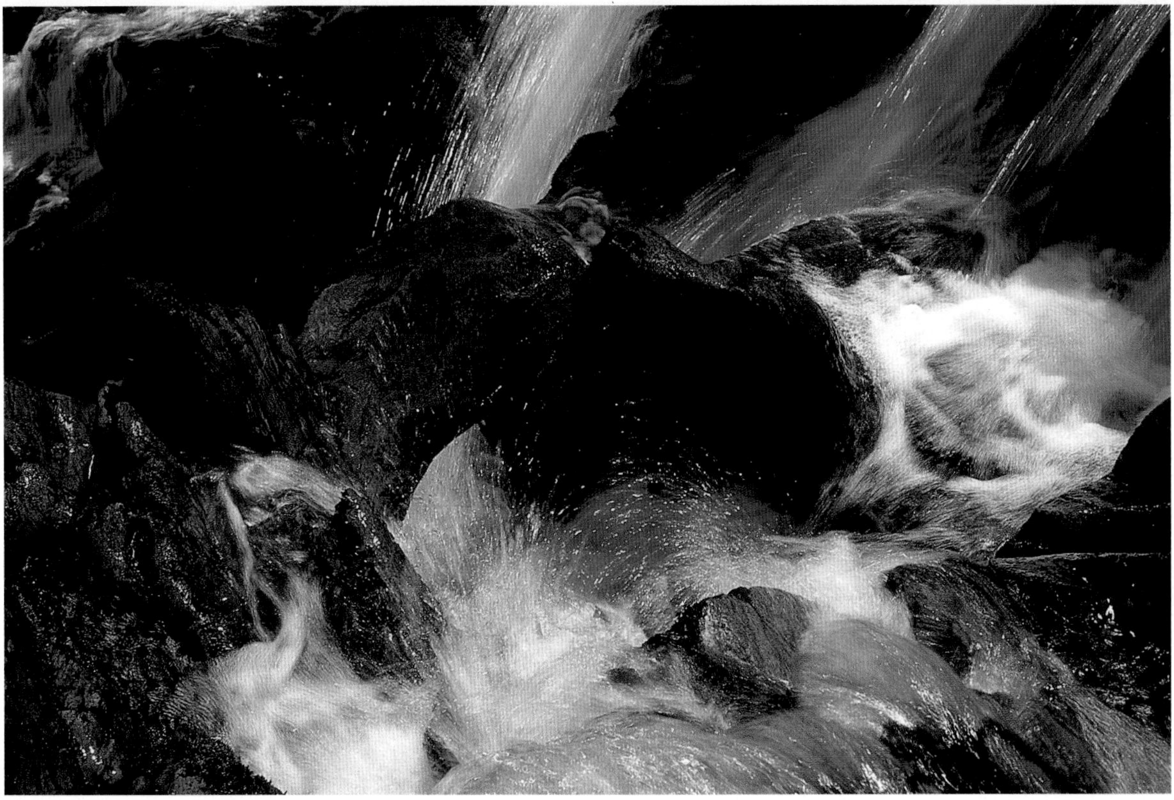

3 Man's influence

Opposite: Llech Idris, a prehistoric standing stone in the remote moorland above Trawsfynydd

Below: The Llyn Celyn reservoir during the 1995 drought. The flooding of the Tryweryn valley between Bala and Trawsfynydd in the 1960s was bitterly opposed by many in Wales

History is an on-going phenomenon – it's very difficult to determine where it all started, and yesterday's news is today's history. We cannot separate our history from our daily lives and in Snowdonia, where the past stares you in the face, the more you experience the place, the more you absorb the heritage. This phenomenon of 'living the heritage' gives the people of the area tremendous resilience in the way they view the world, but it can also be a burden. As with the physical environment of Snowdonia, the challenge is to draw on that legacy and to utilise it to build for the future.

In Snowdonia, the sense of the past is important and new ideas seem to live next to, but not always with, old ones. There is sometimes a bewilderment of conservatism in a radical framework. Its social history is very like its geological history – bold, assertive but complex – and it does hit you in the eye.

The interconnection between geological and human history is profound. Because of its geological foundation, Snowdonia has never been rich in the material sense. The thin acid soils offered little in terms of agricultural wealth, but its mineral reserves have produced pockets of economic prosperity that, within the total historical framework, were short-lived but which were far-reaching in their impact. These pockets of activity also contained the seedbeds of new ideas and it

EXPLORING SLATE COUNTRY

It's not just the big slate quarries that are impressive. There are dozens of sites to be explored, each with its own characteristics and a tale to tell. Visit the Gorseddau Quarry in Cwm Ystradllyn, a scheme that had the pretensions of Penrhyn or Dinorwig but without the quality of slate. Walk along the tramway that was purposely built, and take a detour to see an early example of a factory village, Treforus, built in the 1850s, where each house was semi-detached. As you approach the valley you will not be able to miss the three-floored Ynysypandy Slate Mill. This has been likened to an abbey or an elaborate cotton mill but, whatever the comparison, it has rightly earned the sobriquet 'a monument to a monumental disaster'. It is now a Scheduled Ancient Monument in the care of the Snowdonia National Park Authority and has been investigated and consolidated.

Above: The Penrhyn slate quarry, near Bethesda

Top: Graffiti in the disused Dinorwig quarry above Llyn Peris, referring to the 'Pen Garret Lads' who worked in one of the upper levels of the quarry

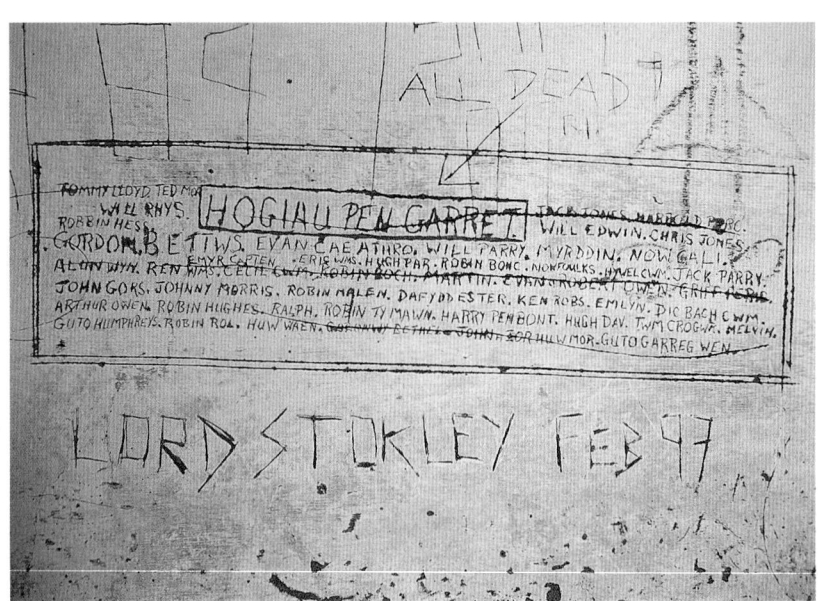

is this juxtaposition – between new and old, between innovation and tradition – that is the essence of the place.

This no more true than with the impact of the Industrial Revolution in Snowdonia, particularly through the legacy of the slate industry. Its impact on the physical landscape is clear to all, but its effect has been equally felt in the cultural landscape of the area. But the main slate areas are outside the National Park boundary. This is because in 1929, when the members of the Addison Committee drew the boundaries of the proposed Park, they deliberately excluded the slate areas. That's why there is a hole in the middle of the Snowdonia National Park where lies Blaenau Ffestiniog. The committee felt that these areas were not beautiful and should be allowed to continue with industrial activity that could be inappropriate for the National Park. In retrospect, this was a double whammy. Slate quarries and their associated tips of waste may not be beautiful in the conventional sense, but they are inextricably linked to the history of the area and, of course, industry need not be incompatible with the environment.

The two big (but not ugly) sisters of the slate industry are Dinorwig at Llanberis and Penrhyn at Bethesda. Penrhyn Quarry is still operational but Dinorwig closed in 1969. From the approach to the summit of Snowdon along the railway line, Dinorwig, with its multi-coloured faces and thick tongues of waste tips, looks impressive, but were you to go down and enter the quarry, the effect would be overwhelming. The site is a series of huge chasms with sheer sides which, when you consider they have been carved out by human hand, are simply awe-inspiring (the North Wales Slate Museum at Llanberis will advise you on accessibility). Both the big quarries employed in total about 5,000 men and between them they produced more than half the total produce of the industry in the nineteenth century

So much of the cultural pattern of the area is because of the slate. Many of the villages hardly existed before the Industrial Revolution, and the names of many of them attest to the nonconformist influence that was such a binding ingredient in their social cement. Biblical names abound, from Bethesda to Nebo, Carmel to Cesarea, where the villages were centred on the newly-built chapel and named after it. These are the new settlements of the nineteenth century and one of the newest, Blaenau Ffestiniog, did not acquire its name until the 1830s. To this new settlement came the new transport system – the railway. By the mid-1880s Blaenau Ffestiniog had three different stations, three different railways and three different gauges in the centre of town. What became known as the London and North Western Railway (LNWR) had been driven through the mountain from the north, with the 2¼-mile tunnel being opened in 1882 (now the Conwy Valley line); the Great Western Railway had stridden over from the east (vestiges remain in the track from the now-closed Nuclear Power Station at Trawsfynydd). Last but not least, the Ffestiniog Railway with its 2ft gauge had been there since 1836.

Some of the railways also served the non-ferrous metal mines of the mountains – the Welsh Highland Railway from Caernarfon to Porthmadog had pretensions in this direction. The copper mines never really fulfilled their owners' dreams and today you can see the remains of their efforts on Snowdon itself. The Miners' Track was to a copper mine above Llyn Glaslyn and today hundreds walk by the mill of the Brittania Mine, consolidated by the National Park Authority.

Before the railways, transport was by road and those, by and large, were awful. Descriptions of their state in the eighteenth and early nineteenth centuries are barely credible even on the main routes. The most famous route through Snowdonia is the A5. By 1836, after Thomas Telford had completed his

Above: The Anglesey Barracks in the ruins of Dinorwig quarry. Here quarry men from Anglesey would live during the week

Below: Ynysypandy slate mill

work, the journey time between London and Holyhead had been reduced from 48 to 27 hours. The Welsh Office has now declared the A5, from Chirk to Bangor, an historical route, which means that any proposed improvements will have to take full account of its essential characteristics. These include the historical features of the road's engineering and road 'furniture' such as milestones, but also significantly environmental considerations – good news for a road that dissects one of Britain's most cherished landscapes.

Presiding over all of this road and rail building and mineral exploitation were the landowners and the entrepeneurs. Snowdonia is peppered by the residences of Victorian businessmen – the exclusive executive housing of the period. These are now hotels, country hotels or perhaps mere hostels. However, the dwellings of the landowners were a different matter – these were and are huge. The neo-Gothic style of Penrhyn Castle, just outside Bangor, the home of Lord Penrhyn, still inspires dread but is now safely in the hands of the National Trust; Y Faenol, home of the Assheton-Smiths of Dinorwig Quarry and one-time owners of Snowdon, is now a training centre; Glynllifon, the home of the Newboroughs who owned land all over Snowdonia, is in the hands of Gwynedd Council, and Plas Tan y Bwlch, a residence of the Oakeley family, owners of the largest quarry in Blaenau Ffestiniog, is now the Snowdonia National Park Study Centre. All of these mansions are surrounded by beautiful gardens and woodlands with two of them, Glynllifon and Faenol, enclosed by miles of walling. Today, these mansions form important assets in the area's heritage. Their extensive grounds, originally private havens of conservation, are now available to the public. These houses are inextricably linked to the quarries and their waste tips – the source of their wealth – and their associated communities with their rows and rows of terraced houses.

Many of the great landowning families emerged after the Act of Union in 1536, when the last vestiges of Welsh law were incorporated into English and the upper classes fell over themselves to be Anglicised. Many benefited from the union with England, not least the Wynns of Gwydir in Dyffryn Conwy. Gwydir Castle in Llanrwst and the recently restored Plas Mawr in Conwy, attest to their good fortune. Those who lost out became the dispossessed, and they are not remembered by fine buildings but in evocative place names.

The south of Snowdonia in the early sixteenth century was the home of the most famous of these dispossessed people, Gwylliaid Cochion Mawddwy – the red-haired outlaws of Mawddwy. As you enter Snowdonia from the direction of Welshpool on the A458 and pass the slate block with the Park's emblem you are entering their territory – Nant y Dugoed (the valley of the dark wood). You soon pass by Llidiart y Barwn where the Gwylliaid took their bloody revenge on the newly-installed authority and ambushed and assassinated the baron who had earlier condemned the Gwylliaid to the gallows. They are still remembered in the pub name at Mallwyd – the Brigands Inn.

Lack of resources has always been a factor in Welsh history, including the Late Medieval Period when Wales was a small, embryonic state facing the wealth and might of a major colonial power. When Edward I finally turned his full attention to Wales in 1280, the little mountainous country had no chance. After Llywelyn II (in Welsh, Llywelyn ein Llyw Olaf, our last leader) was killed in 1282, Edward I set about ensuring that there would be no further trouble from this corner of the kingdom by enclosing the stronghold of Snowdonia through a series of impressive castles. As Frances Lynch says in the CADW guide to Gwynedd: 'He planned one of the most ambitious and expensive campaigns of castle and borough

OWAIN GLYNDWR

Just over a hundred years before the time of the Gwylliaid, there was a much more serious conflict as Owain Glyndwr led a remarkably successful rebellion against the English throne between 1400–1410. From his Parliament in Machynlleth (the Parliament House still stands), he had been in touch with the Pope to get the Welsh church recognised as an independent body, made an agreement with the French and had acquired an ally in England. But the resources of Wales were no match for those of the English Crown and it all came to nothing.

Opposite: The ruins of the Britannia Copper Works in the shadow of Lliwedd

building that Europe had ever seen. Over twelve years he spent £60,000 [about £33 million in today's terms], more than ten times his annual income, on building castles and walled towns at Conwy, Caernarfon, Harlech, and Beaumaris and the refurbishment of Llywelyn's castle at Criccieth. This integrated programme – each borough defended by its castle, and each castle accessible by sea – has left Wales with a legacy of medieval military architecture of truly international importance.'

The Anglo-Norman castles are now being listed as a World Heritage Site and the cultural landscape they have created is as integral to Snowdonia as is the phy-sical landscape of mountain and the sea.

The Welsh had their own castles too – hardly as impressive as the Edwardian models and with quite different reasons for their locations. Welsh castles tend to be sited on important inland routes so the Welsh princes could control trade and communications. Castell y Bere sits in splendid isolation in the Dysynni Valley near Tywyn; Dolbadarn Castle is perched between the two lakes of Padarn and Peris; and Dolwyddelan, traditionally the home of Llywelyn I (Llywelyn Fawr, the Great) and stronghold of his nephew, Llywelyn II, lies at the crossroads between important north-south and east-west routes.

The period leading up to the struggles with the powerful neighbours to the east was one of great activity. The same power game was being played in Wales as in the rest of Europe in the Medieval period, as one family dynasty vied with the other for supremacy. While the aristocrats were playing their war games, commercial life became more and more connected with the monks and brothers of the monastic orders. Indeed, such was their influence that the Early Medieval period has been dubbed the 'Age of the Saints' in Wales. Lines of communication in trade as well as warfare were based around the Irish Sea, which provided a route to continental Europe via the Celtic cousins in Brittany.

Dolbadarn Castle and Llyn Padarn

THE CELT

The whole question of what is meant by 'Celtic' is fascinating and fraught with difficulties. We have no written evidence that they called themselves by that name and of how much of the idea of 'the Celt' is a product of the imagination of Welsh writers of the late Renaissance, who were doing their utmost to show that the Welsh had a claim on Britain. What we do have is a legacy of marvellously-crafted designs on a range of artefacts in the Late Bronze Age/Iron Age that were truly trans-European in character. Many of these are created around motifs based on the triskel, three circles entwined representing the three elements of earth, fire and water. I believe the concept of the Celt evokes the idea of Europe, and perhaps we should think of them as the first Europeans and not as a distinct people.

Opposite (top): Remains of the Cistercian Cymer Abbey near Dolgellau; (below) Llyn Tegid, near Llanuwchllyn

North of Dolgellau is Llanelltyd – the church of St Illtud – and the round churchyard attests to its antiquity; north of Brest in Brittany is the village of Laniltud. Same name, same tradition, similar language. But the tradition of the Celtic Church was based on the hermitage rather than the community, and sites today like Llandecwyn, or Llandanwg, are still in splendid isolation. Returning to Llanelltyd, here we see Abaty Cymer. This Cistercian abbey was founded in 1189–90 with the original mother-house being Clairvaux in Burgundy. The Cistercian monks were largely responsible for building up the sheep trade, as well as being involved in mining and metallurgy.

Before the arrival of the Continental orders, Celtic saints roamed the land. They featured in the period of Arthur and his mythical heroes, whose names are found in places throughout Snowdonia and in one church in particular which is located on the edge of the National Park, called Llandderfel, the church of Derfel. This 'saint', Derfel Gadarn (Derfel the Strong) was a supporter of Arthur and was present at Camlan, and in the church today is his shrine in the form of a carved horse. The church is situated in an area redolent with tradition.

Llandderfel is not far from Y Bala, the village at the edge of the largest natural lake in Wales, Llyn Tegid. Today, Bala is regarded by visitors as a gateway to Snowdonia but it is a remarkably historic place in its own right. A medieval borough was established in 1310, and this can still be seen in the grid pattern of the streets stretching away from Tomen y Bala, the earthwork castle that guarded the town. In 1997 the National Eisteddfod was held on the level Rhiwlas fields at the northern edge of the town, near the hamlet of Llanfor. It was already known that the fields contained Roman military camps, but research instigated by the National Park Authority revealed that the Llanfor area had the remains of a multi-period landscape, with monuments dating from prehistoric times to the nineteenth century.

In Welsh literature, the area has always been associated with a famous poet of the Middle Ages, Llywarch Hen, who referred to a substantial court at 'Llanfawr', and remains of medieval periods were discovered in the 1997 investigation, making it a most appropriate site for Wales' leading cultural festival.

The Romans came, saw and conquered – in AD77 to be precise, and the occupation lasted until AD383. As the Normans did nearly a thousand years later, the Romans ringed Snowdonia with fortifications: Caerhun in the Conwy Valley, Caer Llugwy between Betws y Coed and Capel Curig, and Tomen y Mur near Trawsfynydd. As we have seen at Llanfor, there were numerous military camps scattered throughout the area and without doubt there are more to be discovered. The main base was Segontium at Caernarfon where CADW now has a small but interesting museum.

The Romans built so many forts in and around Snowdonia for the same reasons as did the Anglo-Normans under Edward I: the resistance of the native people in their mountain stronghold. In this case it was the Ordovices, to whom we now assign the term 'Celtic'. It is difficult to decide when the people we call Celts had begun to penetrate what is now Wales, but their presence was well established by 500BC. It has been customary to think of the arrival of the Celts as waves of invasions but this view is now discredited. As Barry Raftery says in the authoritative work, *The Celts* (1991): 'Clearly, the simple invasion model alone is scarcely adequate to explain the complex and multifaceted processes of cultural change which combined, in the course of the last millennium BC, to make the islands "Celtic". Moreover, it is likely that the dominant element in the ethnic composition of the "Celtic" Iron Age population, both in Britain and Ireland, had its roots in the indigenous Bronze Age.'

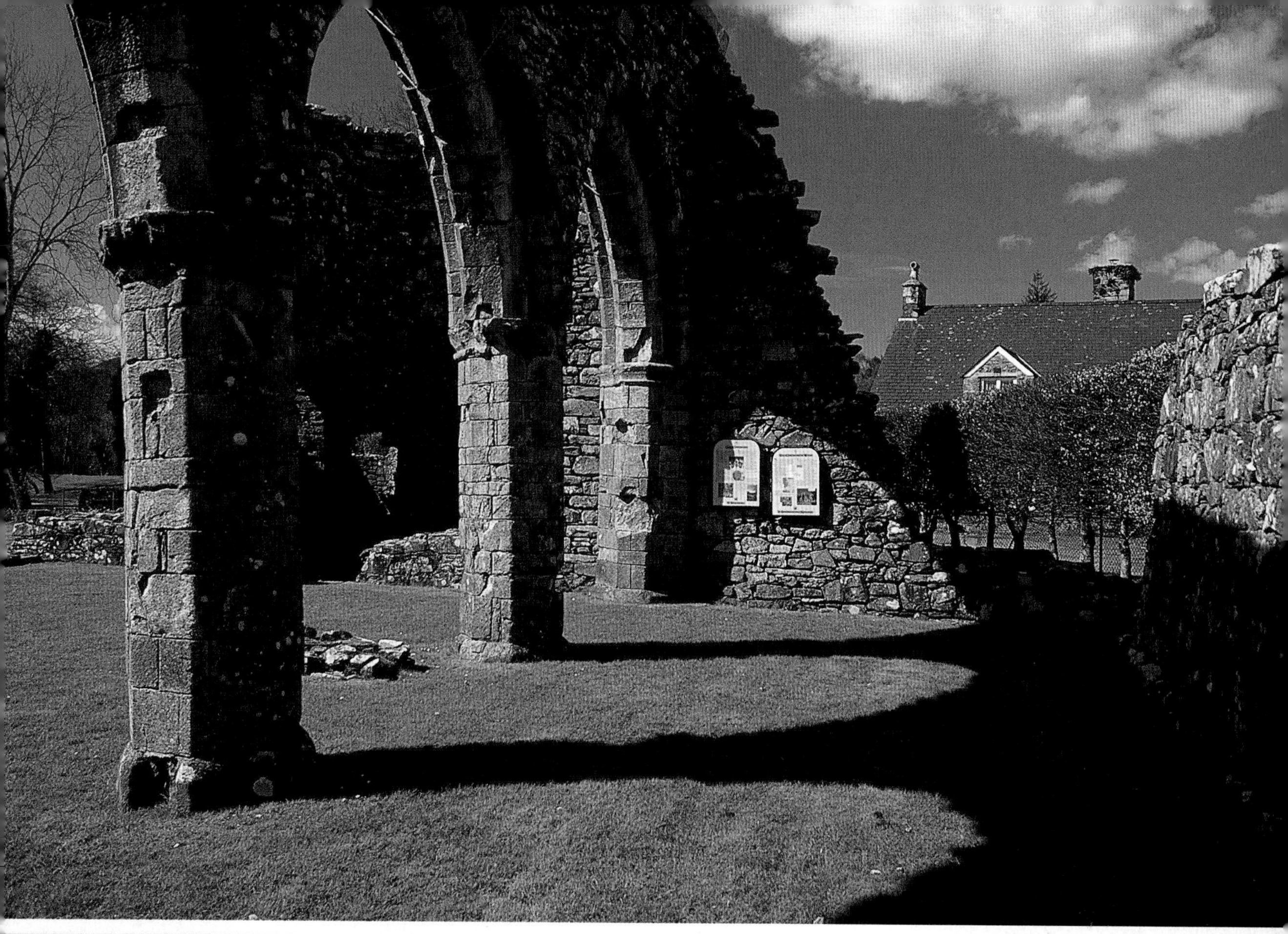

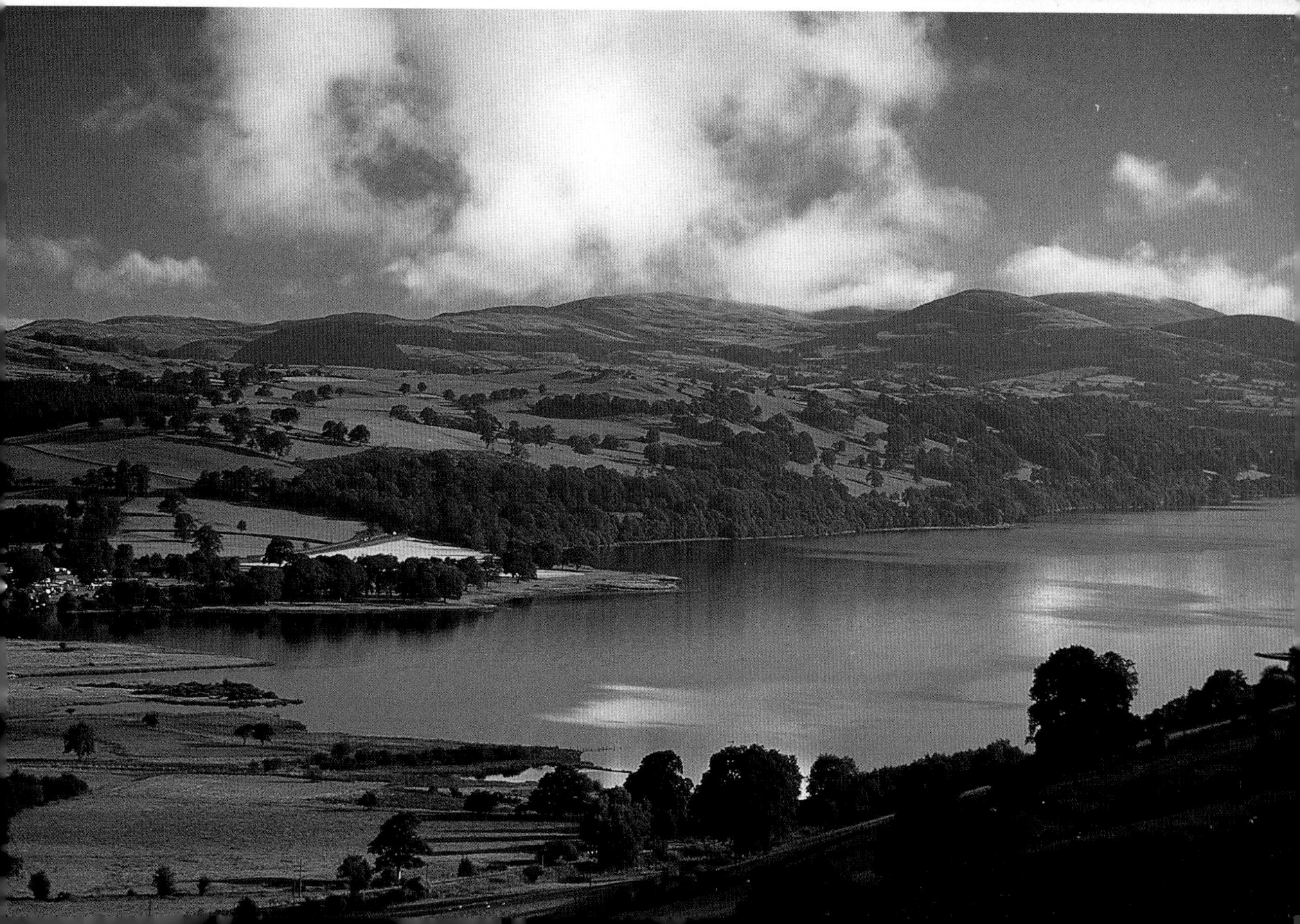

In archaeological/landscape terms the 'Celtic' presence (Romano-British is the preferred archaeological term) is best represented by the hill fort. Perhaps the most spectacular in terms of its archaeology and its location is Pen y Gaer, Llanbedr y Cennin. This site is high above Dyffryn Conwy and is noted for its most dramatic feature – a *chevaux de frise* – an area of densely located small stones designed to seriously hamper unwary attackers, described by Lynch as a sort of Iron Age 'minefield'. Another fascinating site is Bryn y Castell, at Ffestiniog. This has been excavated and partially reconstructed by the National Park Authority and is well worth a visit. It has produced remarkable evidence of iron working and has shown that the people involved were much more sophisticated than was assumed, and that they traded extensively in much of Western Europe. Perhaps the Euro is not such a new thing after all!

As we have seen above, we must dispel the notion that the Iron Age people displaced the Bronze Age inhabitants. What was more likely was the absorption of new ideas and new technology taking over from the old. What we know is that the introduction of iron brought in the new technology. It is thought that many of the folklore tales of Wales which refer to the Tylwyth Teg (the fair people or fairies) being fearful of iron originate in the period when the 'old' people became isolated in their way and retreated from the innovations. Many lakes throughout Wales are associated with versions of a tale about a lady emerging from the waters and bringing wealth in terms of livestock with her, but who would only remain with her lucky man if she was not struck by iron. Did the lady-figure represent the old Bronze Age people, fearful of new materials and technology?

It is somewhat appropriate then that what we associate with the Bronze Age is the burial circles and/or ritual sites. Undoubtedly the jewel in this particular crown is Bryn Cader Faner which has been described by Frances

Tomen y Mur, near Trawsfynydd, consisting of a medieval motte and bailey situated within the walls of a Roman fort

Lynch as 'a monument of simple but brilliantly effective design, placed with sophisticated precision in its dramatic settings so as to achieve maximum impact on travellers approaching from the south. It is arguably the most beautiful Bronze Age monument in Britain.'

Bryn Cader Faner is located on the Dyffryn Ardudwy coastal platform in the hinterland between Harlech and Barmouth. This area positively bristles with monuments and has long been recognised. In 1812, the Reverend John Evans wrote in his substantial tome *The Beauties of England and Wales, Volume XVII* '...perhaps in no part of Britain is there still remaining such an assemblage of relicks belonging to druidical rites and customs as are found in this place.'

Today, we would balk at using the term 'Druidical', which suffers from the tendency to being a catch-all phrase for anything pre-Roman, but the fact remains that this territory bears testimony to thousands of years of human occupation. Perhaps we should not forget its antecedents in folklore. Somewhere here lies Llia'r Gwyddel (Llia the Goidel), a contemporary of Rita Gawr of Snowdon fame. His resting place cannot be far from Llyn Irddyn, a lake that has it own tradition of 'The Lady of the Lake' and her intolerance of iron, and to the Rev John Evans and his contemporaries what were the Tylwyth Teg but 'the souls of the virtuous Druids, who not having been Christians cannot enter the Christian heaven, but enjoy heavens of their own'.

So in Dyffryn Ardudwy we can view and imagine human activity from the Neolithic through the Bronze and Iron Ages, Early and Late Medieval Ages to early Modern and the early twentieth century. A walk from the coast inland to Ceunant Egryn will reveal the Neolithic burial cairn of Carneddau Hengwm; the

Iron Age hillfort of Bryn Dinas; medieval farmsteads and fields; large field walls of the nineteenth-century enclosures, and remains of manganese mining of the first decade of the twentieth century. And looking down from the coastal platform we can view the mid-twentieth century's material evidence of tourism in miles and miles of caravan parks.

The spectacular physical features of Snowdonia play host to spectacular archaeology spreading over at least 5,000 years and, of course, it is the very nature of that environment which allows for the survival of human material remains. Within that continuity represented by archaeology, changes are always occurring. It is fortunate for Snowdonia that the framework for change lies within a National Park that has the promotion of the cultural heritage at its heart. Today in Snowdonia, history is being created within an environment of care even with the occasional adversity.

All through history
The great brush has not rested,
Nor the paint dried; yet what eye,
Looking coolly, or, as we now,
Through the tears' lenses, ever saw,
The work when it was not finished?

'The View from the Window'
by R. S. Thomas

Opposite: (top) Bryn Cader Faner, a burial site situated in the bleak foothills of the Rhinogydd; (below) remains of manganese mining in the Rhinogydd, south of Llyn Cwm Bychan

Part of Carneddau Hengwm, one of the many prehistoric monuments in the Dyffryn Ardudwy area

4 Land use, culture and customs

Above: Valley fog in Nantgwynant

Opposite: Stone walls, field barns and woodland in Cwm Nantcol, all features protected and enhanced by the Tir Cymen/Tir Gofal scheme

How do we evaluate land use in a National Park? Is it a factor of employment or of land management? Do we consider the amount of land utilised for different categories of physical activity such as farming, forestry and mineral/stone extraction and, say, power generation? Or can we argue that the most widespread land use is in fact 'in the eye of the beholder'?

Is it not the case that the simple fact of looking at and experiencing Snowdonia is its most significant land use? The Authority's second main aim is the promotion of the enjoyment of the National Park by ensuring access and means for recreation. This aim applies to everyone, be they resident or non-resident but, most of the time, we link the enjoyment of Snowdonia with tourism. In the chapter on the history of Snowdonia, it was said that one of its essential characteristics was the juxtaposition of the old and the new, and this is most evident in the role that tourism plays today. Many 'new' ideas in terms of tourist facilities and services depend as much on traditional activities as the natural beauty of the area.

The combination of the natural assets, the tradition and then the adaptation to contemporary requirement seems to be working successfully. A visitor survey in 1994 showed that between 6.6 and 10.5 million visitor days were spent in the National Park, and every summer the population of Snowdonia swells from 25,000

EARLY TOURISM

Tourism in itself is not a new industry in Snowdonia. Travellers began to appear in the late eighteenth century and increased in number as the nineteenth century progressed. In the mid-1850s the first of the regular tourist guides appeared, with the classic example being Blacks' Picturesque Guide. Today, when we talk so much about the need for integrated transport, it would be worthwhile looking at these to show it was done over a hundred years ago, and how smoothly the guide combined the sights with the transport network.

Below: Pont Scethin on the old Harlech to Dolgellau coach route, now long abandoned
Opposite: The widely used A487, north of Corris. Over 90 per cent of visitors to Snowdonia every year come by car

to about 80,000. Popular tourist facilities, in or at the edge of the Park, such as the Llechwedd Slate Caverns, Ffestiniog Railway and Portmeirion village each welcome about 200,000 people. But the biggest attraction of them all, with some 500,000 visitors a year, is the summit of Snowdon. As the National Park Authority itself says in its Local Plan 'The natural beauty and landscape of Snowdonia represents the most significant economic resource in the area.'

By 1830 what we now call the A5 was in operation and as A.H. Dodd says in his *Industrial Revolution in North Wales* 'Freed from the menace of ruts, deadly angles and impossible gradients, the highways began to swarm with wheeled vehicles. The pack-horse, pack-mule and sledge gave way to the waggon, and degenerate travellers sought the idle discomfort of the stage coach or post-chaise instead of riding their own horse.'

The significance of the A5 has now been acknowledged and as stated previously, it has been officially declared an 'Historical Route' from Chirk to Bangor, which means that its historical and environmental qualities will now be protected. This may pose some questions about what to do about the serious traffic congestion problems that occur along it and other routes in the summer. In early 1999 the National Park Authority published a study of the transport issue called *The Snowdonia Northern Area Study*. This concluded that 'to leave things as they are is not an option' and recommended defining towns as 'gateways' to Snowdonia where people can park their cars and transfer to buses. Parking in the core would be discouraged by charging excessive prices, and money would be invested in providing a full public service. A scheme of this nature will have to be put into operation or Snowdonia, like other National Parks, will choke on its own popularity.

Caravan parks north of Barmouth, which for many are viewed as the unacceptable face of tourism

Which brings us to one of the conundrums of tourism in Snowdonia – its seasonality. The Wales Tourist Board estimate that nearly 70 per cent of the trade occurs in the three summer months. As one who lives in Snowdonia, the correlation between numbers of visitors and school holidays is clear to see. Thus for three months of 'the season' the roads are packed, cars parked in all corners, queues of motors, coaches and people form and re-form. Come September, the contrast is clear. This not only creates problems for tourist operators but also for the National Park Authority as evidenced in the transport study mentioned above. Attempts are being made to extend the 'season', such as via the Mid-Wales Festival of the Countryside, which provides information about places, facilities and events, and according to Dr David Bellamy, its chairman, the Festival has extended the season by a month.

The challenge is to have sustainable tourism, which means benefiting from the environment without exploiting it and providing all-year economic sustenance to the community. This is being achieved in Portmeirion village, the architectural creation of Sir Clough Williams-Ellis in 1926, who was also one of the founders of the National Park movement in the 1930s and 1940s. It seems fully appropriate that his dream lives on and his village and Snowdonia take their place in establishing models for the green tourism of the modern age.

However, one major drawback in achieving such green tourism is the fact that over 90 per cent of the visitors to Snowdonia arrive by car, when many could easily reach the place by train. If more people came by rail, it would certainly ease some of the problems highlighted by the Northern Snowdonia Study. The network may be not what it was, but the links are there. Betws y Coed can be reached with the Conwy Valley line connection to the main London-Holyhead line, and Tywyn,

Barmouth and Porthmadog are on the Cambrian Coast line. Within the Park there are a number of narrow gauge railways, of course, the most famous being the Ffestiniog Railway connecting Blaenau Ffestiniog with Porthmadog, and thus the Conwy line with the Cambrian Coast.

The original reasons for the building of these railways were mainly to do with the need to transport stone and minerals from the mountains to the sea and to destinations in urban Britain. But the Welsh Highland Railway from Caernarfon to Porthmadog was inaugurated in the 1930s just when most of the quarries and mines it was supposed to serve had closed! Today, the trackbed is used for walking, especially in the Beddgelert area, but a decision in 1999 to allow it to be reopened poses many questions for the National Park Authority.

Above: Portmeirion – a model for sustainable tourism?

Below: Ready for work on the Snowdon Mountain Railway

Many questions arise also with some of the traditional land uses of Snowdonia – mining and quarrying. The importance of slate to the economic geology and history was described in the Introduction and Chapter 1, and we must remember that the activity continues in Bethesda and Blaenau Ffestiniog and near Corris in the south, with the slate quarries of Penrhyn, Ffestiniog, Cwt y Bugail, Llechwedd and Aberllefenni employing around 500 men in all. There was no mineral extraction occurring in 1999 as the one gold mine that was operational, Gwynfynydd near Ganllwyd, closed in April of that year. Closed with the gold mine were the tourist trips from Dolgellau to the mine as well as the Welsh Gold Centre at the Marian.

This slate quarry at Aberllefenni, near Corris, specialises in larger pieces of slate not produced elsewhere in Wales

Gold mining has been an intermittent activity from when it was discovered in Dyffryn Mawddach in 1854 and, you never know, the lure of the yellow metal might yet prove strong enough to suck more money into the Snowdonia hills.

The connection between mining and tourism is an interesting one. In the early eighteenth century, Lord Penrhyn erected pagodas in his quarry on Moel Elidir so that the better class of people could look at the poorer class of people creating their wealth for them by ripping the slate out of the hillside. Transport links were also in the first place primarily for the quarries, but in some cases accommodated tourists. The link between quarrying and transport is still there but the relationship has been totally reversed.

Another traditional activity which is changing its pattern is the production of power. Water has played a key part with many of the slate quarries dependant on water wheels to drive their machinery. In the early part of the twentieth century, water was utilised to produce electricity and the Cwm Dyli Hydro Electric Station was opened in 1906, and at Maentwrog in 1928. Today, the tradition continues with the Ffestiniog and Dinorwig Pumped Storage Schemes but also, under a Government inducement scheme for renewable energy, many smaller projects are being put forward. Cwm Croesor's original plant of 1906 is being rebuilt and a small plant will appear in Hafod y Llan just off the Watkin Path to Snowdon.

Even though the production of renewable energy is to be welcomed, it is not without its problems. In terms of hydro power, there are serious drawbacks with what are called 'run-of-the-river' schemes. These draw water directly out of the stream and can thus threaten the ecology of the river bed and valley. Another renewable energy option that poses a conundrum is wind energy. Wind power stations have a distinct impact on the landscape, for a small amount of electrical output. While up to now none has been proposed within the National Park, there are a number of possible sites around the edges which would seriously detract from the quality of the experience of the Park were they to be erected.

But the truly renewable resources of Snowdonia are to be found in the grasslands of the farming industry, the trees of the forestry industry and above all, in the character of its people. As mentioned on page 60, the people of Trawsfynydd, after losing their economic lifeline, are now deploying their ingenuity to recreate the economic base. Forestry and farming, the two mainstays of visible land use, are also reassessing their situation.

Of the 221,000 hectares of the National Park, around 36,754 hectares, or 17 per cent, have tree cover. Of that tree cover 14 per cent is coniferous and 3 per cent deciduous. Most of the woodlands are Forestry Commission plantations, but the value of trees as contributors to the landscape is acknowledged in the fact that much of two forest estates have been designated forest parks – these are the Coed y Brenin and Gwydir Forests. What that means is that parts of these forests can be managed for amenity and recreation as well as for timber and, in fact, in certain areas, the amenity value of the trees has complete precedence. To savour the experience of trees in the landscape, visit the Ty'n ŷ Groes picnic site near Ganllwyd and wander through the inspiring stands of Douglas firs on the side of the Mawddach.

Maturing Douglas firs in the Coed y Brenin Forest Park

MONUMENT TO CREDULITY

The great monument to non-fossil fuel energy in Snowdonia is the now closed Trawsfynydd Nuclear Station, which was opened in 1953. It strains our credulity today that this huge mass of concrete could have been placed in one of the most open areas of Snowdonia to produce power with a fuel that would leave behind a radioactive presence for untold years. The question of what to do with the core of the reactors and other waste products is a huge dilemma for the National Park and the National Assembly for Wales. Nevertheless the power station employed hundreds of people and brought in substantial financial benefit for the forty or so years of its existence, and its closure left a huge gap in the local economy. Efforts are being made at Trawsfynydd to capitalise on the site and the lake for tourism.

Llyn Trawsfynydd, with Moelwyn and Snowdon in the background, with the nuclear power station on the right of the picture

Above: Near Trawsfynydd. Sheep farming is a precarious occupation in some parts of Snowdonia
Left: Dry-stone walling in Cwm Nantcol
Below: Intensively managed fields in Cwm Nantcol. Agricultural 'improvement' can threaten biodiversity

The deciduous trees are almost entirely amenity woodlands, the outstanding example being in Dyffryn Maentwrog. These woodlands are now in the care of the Countryside Council for Wales but owe their existence and their survival to the Oakeley family of Plas Tan y Bwlch, who managed them for the production of timber ribs for the Porthmadog ships of the last century.

The demands of change are nowhere more keenly felt than in the base industry of Snowdonia – farming. There are some 1,500 registered holdings occupying some 80 per cent of the land area and employing 3,000 farmers and farm workers. The farms are in the main small family units, entirely involved in livestock rearing. For over fifty years they have been driven by subsidies which put maximising food production above all else. This resulted in heavier grazing in some areas, as well as an over-dependence on a limited product range. The system is gradually becoming less conducive to maintaining people on farms and in the countryside. As subsidies are squeezed, more and more farms are amalgamated leading to a 'worst of two worlds' situation – less valuable ecology and less cultural diversity.

The raw material of the tourist industry in Snowdonia is not only the land but the people and their cultures. It is absolutely crucial that the distinctive culture is maintained as a living, organic entity in itself because were such a culture exploited and subverted simply for the needs of the tourist, it would never be replaced. Cultural diversity is much more difficult to replace than biodiversity.

It is important to realise that the old cultural patterns are disappearing and new ones emerging. Snowdonia still suffers from the loss of young people, but the ones

Opposite: The mixed forestry and farming landscape north of Dolgellau

TIR CYMEN

Tir Cymen, the land-use agric-environment experiment conducted from the early 1990s by the National Park Authority and CCW in one part of Snowdonia, was vitally important. Farmers who participated entered their whole farm into a management agreement administered by the Park Authority, in which they adopted more environmentally-friendly practices, allowed access to the open areas of their farms, and sometimes reduced numbers of stock. In return, they received whole-farm payments and a commercial rate for maintaining and improving historical and biological features, as well as looking after footpaths. This was a tremendous success and in 1999, a new, all-Wales

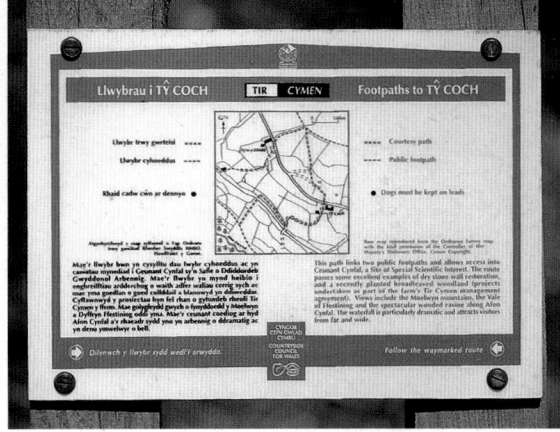

scheme called 'Tir Gofal' (cared-for landscape) was launched.

Tir Cymen/Gofal points the way forward for a more balanced agriculture and also links in with tourism as do so many other economic sectors. In terms of the kind of activities encouraged by the National Park, tourism is not so much an industry in itself but a by-product of other activities. The intense variety of habitats which characterises Snowdonia is a factor of the physical characteristics modified by generations of land management for the production of primary raw material, such as food, timber and stone.

Therefore it is crucial that such activities are continued and that is why the duty placed on National Parks in 1995 to foster the socio-economic well-being of local communities is so important.

Left: Striking forest and mountain scenery north of Dolgellau

THE WELSH LANGUAGE

The most distinctive cultural feature associated with Snowdonia is the Welsh language. Today, about 65 per cent speak Welsh, but a hundred years ago 90 per cent of the people of Snowdonia spoke Welsh only. This is a marvellous phenomenon when we consider the proximity of Wales to England, the comparative sizes of their population (approximately 3 million against 50 million) and the strength of the English language. In fact, when Henry VIII annexed Wales to England with the Act of Union in 1536, the Welsh language was to be eradicated. We must be clear that this was to be in 'official' use only and ironically, Henry's daughter, Elizabeth I, passed a law to translate the Bible into Welsh in 1576, and through that ensured the survival of the language. The person responsible for the translation, Bishop Morgan lived in Snowdonia, in Ty Mawr, Wybrnant, now in the possession of the National Trust.

The effects of the 1536 legislation led to the Welsh language becoming the language of home and hearth and English becoming the language of state and business. In the eighteenth and nineteenth centuries, this dichotomy was deepened as the language of the nonconformist movement was Welsh and the language became identified with the chapel. The established church retained English as its language. Thus the religious division of language further reinforced the class division, with the workers going to the chapels and the landowners and the rich attending church. In late nineteenth-century literature, the dynamism of the Welsh language in Snowdonia was channelled into religious texts but also, interestingly, into quite radical political texts. It is from this background that David Lloyd George emerged to lead the British Empire. However, following World War I and the depressions of the thirties and then World War II, the language declined remarkably, as did the energy that was so evident in the society at the beginning of the century.

Today, things have changed for the better, especially since the Welsh Language Act of 1993. Some of the energy has returned and now the Welsh language is on a par with English and the National Park Authority itself conducts its business in both languages, but with Welsh being the most prominent.

that remain are much more conscious of the value of their language and culture as expressed in a modern mode. If you are fortunate enough to be in Dolgellau at the beginning of July call in at 'Y Sesiwn Fawr', when the centre of the town is closed to traffic and Eldon Square is transformed into a festival site of Celtic music from all over Western Europe. At any time of the year you can hear Welsh pop groups 'doing their stuff' in Welsh and in English. Generally, people are becoming more self-confident in their identity and that will certainly be reinforced in the National Assembly.

This metamorphosis is reflected in changes in the material culture. We see the social buildings of the early twentieth century, the chapels, being converted for other uses such as garages and art galleries, or being demolished. The new social buildings are the leisure centres such as Tywyn, Dolgellau, Bala, Porthmadog and Penygroes. These are now the 'chapels' at the change of the millennium, as people flock to them to 'worship' on a Sunday.

But culture and language do not exist in a vacuum – they occur in a socio-economic context. The 1995 Environment Act altered the aims of National Parks to include the protection and enhancement of culture which, coupled to the duty of the National Park to 'foster the economic and social well-being' of the area, reinforces the need for a programme of sustainable development.

Snowdonia has been designated for its landscape qualities but in addition to that some 20 per cent of its land area is under nature conservation designation as Sites of Special Scientific Interest and National Nature Reserves. In fact, Snowdonia has the highest density of nature conservation designations in Europe. The outstanding quality of the area is, perhaps, reflected in the fact that the National Trust is a major landowner with about 9 per cent of Snowdonia (including much of Snowdon itself) in its possession. Other conservation agencies have interests as well, such as the RSPB and the Wildlife Trusts.

The tremendous variety and richness in terms of landscape and biodiversity has been a feature of indigenous Welsh folklore and literature from time immemorial. The poetry and literature of locally-born but nationally-important writers resound with the intimacy of the natural and the infinite questions of the human's role in the cosmos. Many are able, like William Blake:

> *To see a world in a grain of sand*
> *And a heaven in a Wild Flower*
> *Hold Infinity in the Palm of your hand*
> *And Eternity in an Hour.*

And, of course, they see it through the window of the Welsh language. In the twentieth century we can refer to giants such as T.H. Parry Williams of Rhyd Ddu, R. Williams Parry of Penygroes, Gerallt Lloyd Owen of Caernarfon, Gwyn Thomas of Blaenau Ffestiniog, Myrddin ap Dafydd of Llanrwst. The list goes on and continues to grow as young poets take their place in this pantheon. And in the

Vernacular architecture in Cwm Nantcol

English language, living in the area is a giant of the giants, R. S. Thomas.

In the work of each of these poets can be discerned the essentially Celtic trait of sensitivity to landscape and their immediate world. Throughout this guide, reference is made to place names and some of their associated tales – there is hardly a hill, mountain, lake or stream that does not have a story to tell. The tradition continues but each generation redefines the relationship. The poets named above represent at least three generations but they, in fact, span countless generations as they produce literature with its roots deep in the rocks of Snowdonia and its people. As Sir John Rhys said in his seminal work *Celtic Folklore* in 1904, when he referred to the 'etymologist' who investigates the sources of words (as poets use words to search for sources of ideas):

> *He required the topography – he requires it still, and hence the work of the local etymologist – to connote story or history: he must have something that will import the cold light of physical nature, river and lake, moor and mountain, a warmer tint, a dash of the pathetic element, a touch of the human, borrowed from the light and shade of the world of imagination and fancy which he lives and dreams.*

5 Recreation

Opposite: (top) Runners in the Ras Mynydd Pedol Peris (Peris Horseshoe Mountain Race) reaching the summit of Y Garn; (below) paragliding above Harlech beach, with the Llŷn Peninsula on the horizon

The second main aim of the National Park Authority is underpinned by three important components – access, enjoyment and understanding. Of course, people have been walking, enjoying and appreciating Snowdonia for generations before the National Park concept was ever imagined. Perhaps the greatest change over the years has been in the number of visitors, and this is why such great emphasis has to be put on management and agreement.

And here lies one of the conundrums of tourism in Snowdonia – you pay to visit the tourist facilities, but you walk up Snowdon and every other mountain for free. The greatest assets of Snowdonia – the quality of its landscape – is not owned by anyone, it is what we call a 'public good'. Scenery, views, experience of open countryside, are available to all and are absolutely essential for the health of our society. It is just as essential that all of us can have access to the mountains or public footpaths or through agreement, whoever owns the land. This is the essence of the second aim of National Parks – the encouragement of access to enjoy the countryside.

For many years, interest in the mountains was based around the researches and discoveries of the botanists, and none more so than the Rev William Bingley who published his book on North Wales in 1804. For equipment, he and his guide on Snowdon had 'a small basket to contain our provisions, and hold the roots of such plants as wished to transfer to his garden'.

It was a good thing that there were not too many who followed that practice, and we can be fairly confident that the amateur ecologists of today would not contemplate transferring plants to gardens.

Above the clouds on Tryfan during a winter temperature inversion. Cader Idris can be seen on the horizon

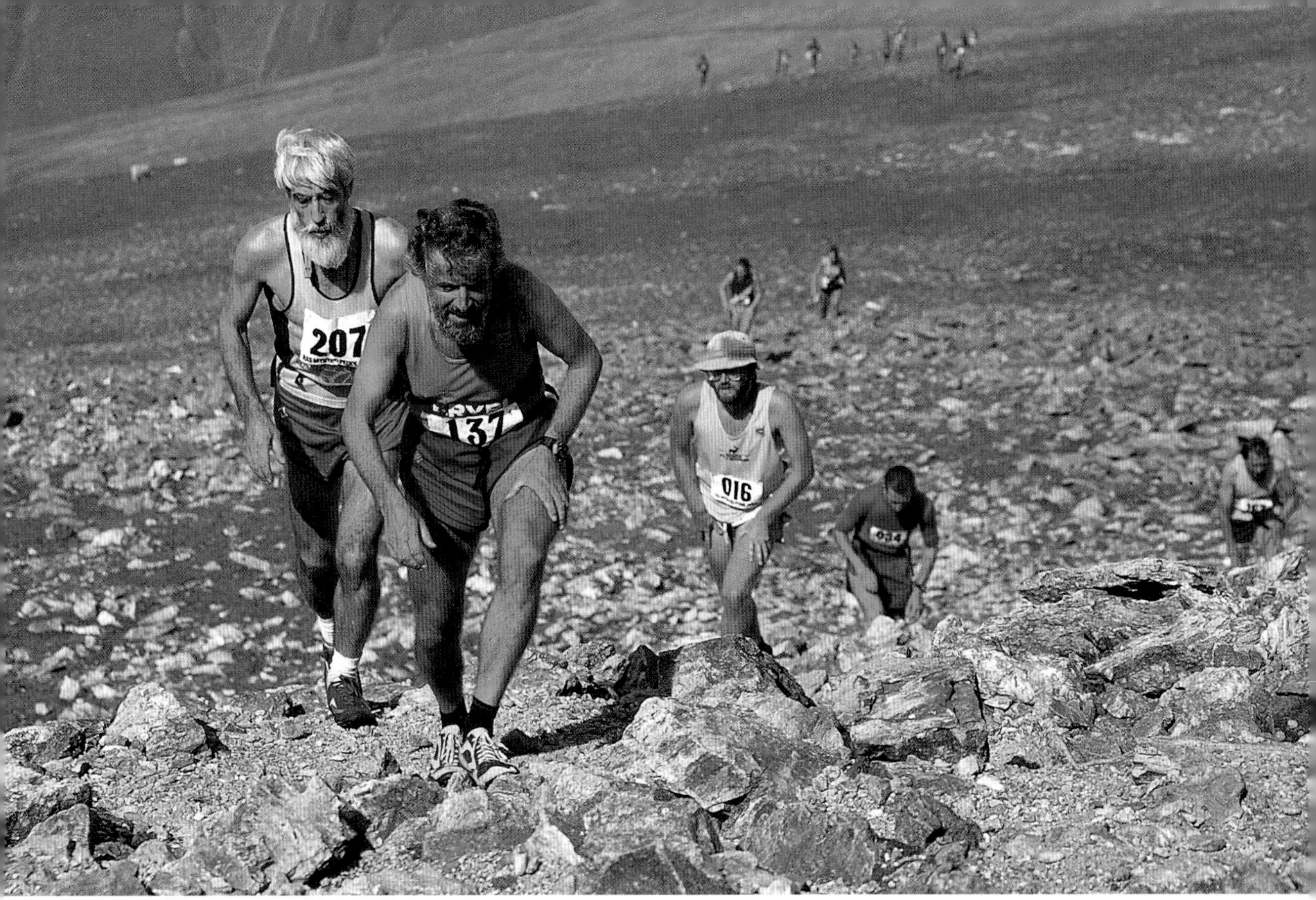
207
137
016

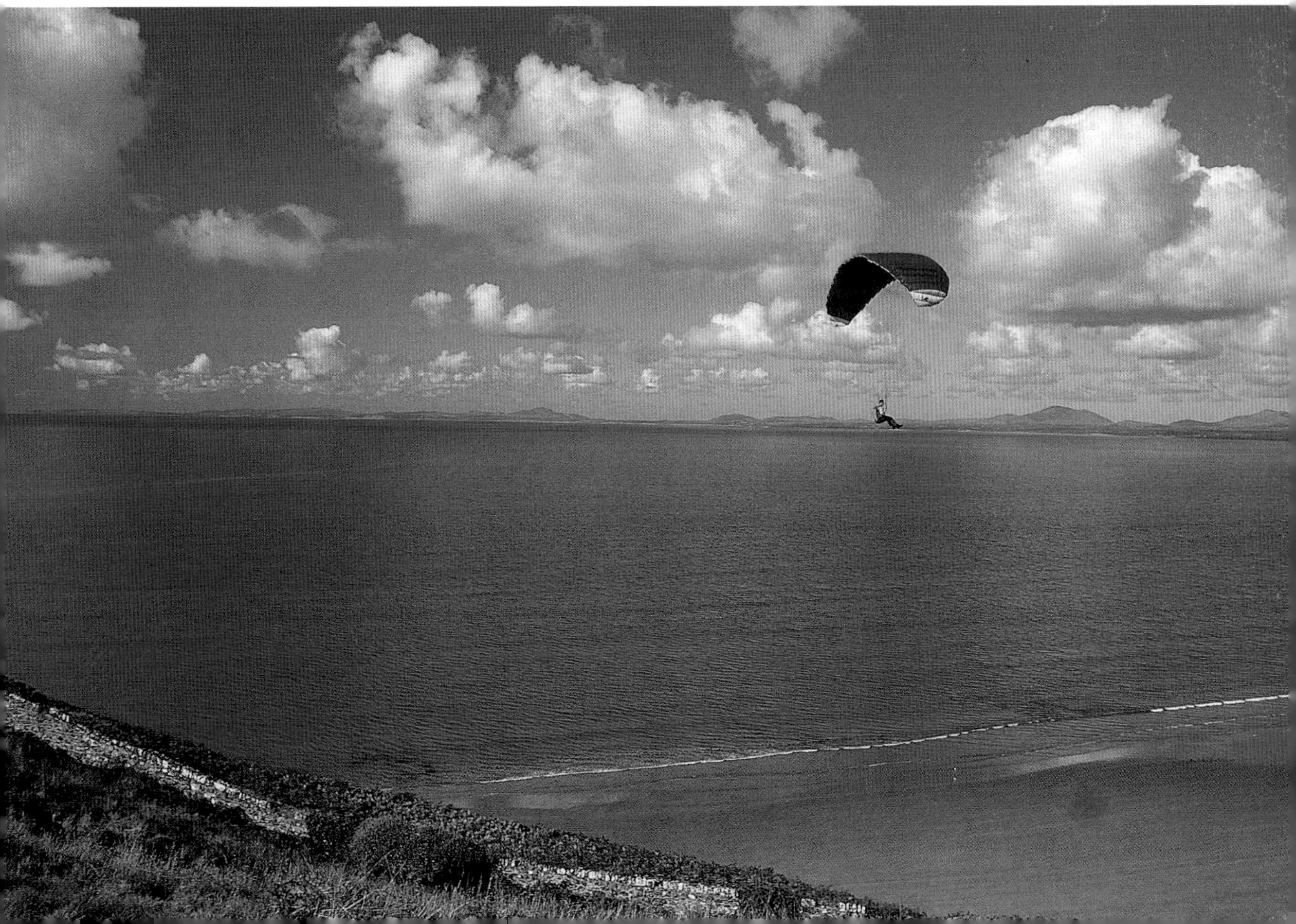

THE FATHER OF CAMBRIAN TOURISTS

The privileged few began to discover Snowdonia in the late eighteenth century. The most famous traveller at this time was Thomas Pennant, the 'Father of Cambrian Tourists'. Pennant wrote his magnificent work, A Tour in Wales in 1783, and in it he describes his ascent of Snowdon in time to welcome the next day:

'The night was remarkably fine and starry: towards morn, the stars faded away, and left a short interval of darkness, which was soon dispersed by the dawn of day. The body of the sun appeared most distinct, with the rotundity of the moon, before it rose high enough to render its beams too brilliant for our sight. The seas which bounded the western part was gilt by its beams, first in slender streaks, at length glowed with redness. The prospect was disclosed to us like the gradual drawing up of curtain in a theatre.'

It was not long after that when Wordsworth, the doyen of the Romantics and spiritual father of the National Park movement, included a climb up Snowdon in his Prelude in 1805, when he also made the ascent at night:

I looked about, and lo!
The Moon stood naked in the
*   heavens, at height*
Immense above my head, and on
*   the shore*
I found myself of a huge sea of mist,
Which, meek and silent, rested at
*   my feet.*

All those who love Snowdonia and Snowdon in particular should experience dawn on the summit. We might not be able to write the poetry, but we can still savour the experience.

But it was George Borrow who could be classed as the first populariser of Snowdonia with his *Wild Wales*, published in 1862. He said that Snowdon was 'interesting on various accounts', namely its picturesque beauty and connection with history. And he adds 'But it is from its connection with romance that Snowdon derives its chief interest.'

It is interesting to note how George Borrow differentiated between beauty and romance, which today we would call folklore. Borrow, who had learnt Welsh, emphasises the importance of Snowdon to the people: 'To the Welsh, besides being the hill of the Awen or Muse, it has always been the hill of hills, the loftiest of all the mountains, the one whose snow is the coldest, the climb to whose peak is the most difficult of all feats; and the one whose fall will be the most astounding catastrophe of the last day.'

But Snowdon, as all other mountains, has other sources of myths and legends and other pantheons to draw upon, not least being the rock climbing fraternity. It is said that it was while naturalising with Bingley on Clogwyn Du'r Arddu that we have the first recorded ascent of bare rock on that famous face – and that was by a Welshman. The Reverend Peter Bailey Williams, Rector of Llanrug and Llanberis, led a climb on that famous face in 1787 – and the rest, they say, is history.

Off-road cycling is also becoming increasingly popular. This activity shows how significant the forestry areas can be in absorbing numbers and relieving pressure, with Coed y Brenin and Gwydir Forests having made special provision for cycling in secluded and beautiful surroundings. The Welsh National Cycle Route, Lôn Las Cymru, also passes through the National Park and offers more relaxing riding.

The more traditional mode of transport, the horse, is also popular and there are pony trekking facilities near Dolgellau and Porthmadog.

The coast is also easily available for all kinds of activities. There are marinas at Pwllheli, Caernarfon and Conwy, mooring facilities at Porthmadog, and you can also avail yourself of the facilities at the National Water Sports Centre at Plas Menai, between Caernarfon and Bangor. Inland, canoeists can enjoy mountain lakes and rivers and go white-water surfing from the National White Water Centre, Canolfan Tryweryn, near Bala.

But the real water sport of Snowdonia is fishing. Fishing for brown trout on the mountain lakes and rivers of Snowdonia must be the ultimate for the fly-

fisherman's art, and fishing the lower rivers for salmon and sewin is as esoteric as it is compulsive.

For all these activities and just simply strolling in the countryside, people have always flocked to the area and have been welcomed. They have enjoyed *de facto* rights of walking in open countryside throughout the Park, and access in general has not been a major issue. Where a dispute did come to a head in the 1980s on the Aran ridge – Aran Benllyn and Aran Fawddwy, west of Bala – the National Park Authority was able to broker a solution. Permissive rights of way were negotiated with the farmers and three acknowledged access points were established to the ridge. Later, the Tir Cymen scheme catered for access on the Arans.

Nevertheless, there is still some resentment within the farming communities when they have to cope with the increasing pressure in their land, especially in the northern area of the Park where the pressure is greatest.

The question is often asked, who pays for the wear and tear? When a farmer sees sheep walking across his hill, he is counting the economic worth of each animal; when he sees walkers, he might well be counting the cost of maintaining walls, stiles and the other furniture of access. That is why the land use experiment conducted in one part of Snowdonia by the National Park Authority and CCW from the early 1990s was so important. The Tir Cymen project has already been described, and in 1999 its successor, Tir Gofal, was launched.

In March 1999 the Labour Government announced it would introduce legislation for the right to roam in open countryside, 'when parliamentary time allows'. In terms of extending access in Snowdonia, the proposed bill would make little difference and, in fact, some people argued that it could be counter-productive as

Above: Moorings in the Artro estuary near Llanbedr

Opposite: Walkers on the Pinnacles, Crib Goch, part of the Snowdon Horseshoe

THE CHALLENGE OF SNOWDONIA

Walking and climbing remained for many years the delight of the rich and privileged. It took new working conditions, education and the train to make walking and climbing more popular activities.

In the late forties, as the National Parks and Access to the Countryside Bill was making its way through Parliament, North could say in his book Snowdonia: 'The rock climbers have built-up, at Pen y Pass and Pen y Gwryd, a long tradition of their particular brand of intellectual and at one time almost monastic athleticism, and it seems the sport, or art, more or less originated on Snowdon and was thence transplanted to the Alps.'

One wonders what the luridly clad, sylph-like figures lingering in the cafés of Llanberis and Tremadog would make of that today. Nevertheless, it's fair to say that Pen y Gwryd certainly played an important part in the history of climbing, serving as the training base of the Everest-conquering team of 1953. What is important is that the sport keeps on changing and developing and producing new challenges – and it is an important function of the Snowdonia National Park. It is no accident that the National Mountain Centre is at Plas y Brenin, Capel Curig.

Today, those challenges are many and varied. Now people not only cling to rocks but also glide off them, as hang-gliding has become popular in many parts of the Park.

The magnificent precipice of Clogwyn Du'r Arddu, on Snowdon – the site of the first rock climb in Wales

some farmers would resent what they see as a betrayal of the understanding and tolerance that had been the norm over the years.

However, the working relationship between the farming and the visiting communities is set to grow as they all appreciate more and more how much they depend on each other. Much public money goes into the countryside and whereas it may not pay directly for the splendours of the landscape it goes a long way towards maintaining the mechanisms that nurture that landscape. As ever, the traditional must live with the innovative, and history shows that it will work.

Below are a series of suggested walks which give a taste of Snowdonia from north to south and west to east. They only give the briefest of descriptions as there are numerous guides and pamphlets for the interested walker.

The main routes up Snowdon, the highest point in the National Park, are the Railway Path from Llanberis; the Miners' Track and PYG Track from Pen y Pass; the Watkin Path from Nant Gwynant; and the Rangers' Path from Llyn Cwellyn.

If you cannot manage the climb to the summit, then take the Miners' Track from Pen y Pass and walk along the well-made track, past Llyn Llydaw and on to Llyn Glaslyn and then return.

The best way to tackle Snowdon is to park your car away from the summit (and Pen y Pass) and use the excellent Snowdon Sherpa Service to pick you up from one side of the mountain and return you to the same place whichever route you may decide to use to descend. The Snowdon Sherpa service runs from towns such as Caernarfon and Porthmadog.

The Pyg track on Snowdon, part of the footpath consolidation work by the National Park

Opposite: The hills south of Dolgellau, with the Aran ridge in the background. The visually intrusive housing development is surprising in a National Park

Abergwyngregin is a secluded wooded valley 7 miles east of Bangor which combines tranquillity with excitement. The valley represents a sharp descent from the wilds of the northern Carneddau range to the Menai Strait – truly between the mountains and the sea. The distance from the car park at Bontnewydd to Aber Falls is less than mile, and there is a well-made track and then a path all the way to the foot of the falls.

There are waymarked footpaths which provide circular routes through the forest plantations on the eastern side of the valley. Some of these are steep in places and can be quite slippery, but they are rewarding as they give good views down the Aber Valley National Nature Reserve, which is managed by the CCW and the Forestry Commission. There is a short trail for disabled people close to the car park.

Dyffryn Ffestiniog is the valley used by the Ffestiniog Railway to take the slates from the mountain to the sea. The railway still runs between Blaenau Ffestiniog and Porthmadog, and provides a great opportunity to reach and return from any number of walks in this remarkable valley.

At the centre of the valley is the Snowdonia National Park Study Centre, Plas Tan y Bwlch, and from its car park visitors can use a large network of footpaths through the amenity woodlands up to Llyn Mair and then through the forestry plantations.

Above: The Mawddach valley from the Precipice Walk

Opposite: Castell y Bere in its secluded location at the head of the Dysynni valley

To experience the area fully, take a train from Porthmadog to Tanygrisiau, the last stop before Blaenau Ffestiniog. Walk from the station and round Llyn Stwlan to pick up the old Ffestiniog Railway trackbed which will bring you to Dduallt Station. Go over the line and followed the waymarked path through Maentwrog woodlands all the way to Llyn Mair. At that point you can go up from the lake to catch the train at Tan y Bwlch Station.

The Precipice Walk 3 miles north of Dolgellau is a spectacular route which provides stupendous views of the mountains around Dyffryn Mawddach with very little climbing. Start from the National Park car park near Llanfachreth. The 3-mile path is narrow in places and is not recommended if you suffer from vertigo. But it is easy to follow as it encircles Moel Cynwch and Moel Faner, providing views to Snowdon and Cader Idris. It is Dyffryn Mawddach, the estuary of the Mawddach, however, that makes this walk.

Arguably, Cader Idris is the best-known mountain in the National Park after Snowdon. In fact, it is not so much a mountain as a long, upstanding ridge that forms the southern sentinel of Snowdonia. There are five peaks on the ridge – from the east Gau Graig, Mynydd Moel, Pen y Gader, Cyfrwy and Tyrau Mawr. In addition, there is the south spur from the summit that leads to Mynydd Pencoed on the Talyllyn Route.

The highest point is Pen y Gader (2,927ft/892m) and this can be reached from the north via the Pony Track, which starts from the National Park car park at Tŷ Nant. From the south, there is a shorter but steeper ascent from Minffordd, in the Talyllyn Valley. Again the start is from a National Park car park, and the climb via Cwm Cau is breathtaking in more ways than one.

Another option is to walk the eastern end of the ridge from Bwlch Tal y Llyn climbing up into Tyrau Mawr; from there along to Mynydd Moel; then Pen y Gader, descending down to Minffordd via Cwm Cau to pick up a service bus to return to the car at the top of the pass. You should allow about five hours for this walk.

The walk from Abergynolwyn to the Dysynni Valley offers an easy glimpse into the character of the southern borders of Snowdonia. Here the hills are slightly more rounded and the land seems more yielding than further north. The walk takes in Castell y Bere, a Welsh castle associated with Llywelyn I.

The three- to four-hour walk from Beddgelert to the Aberglaslyn Pass, via Cwm Bychan and Sygun, takes in many different characteristics of the heart of Snowdonia. Views include the Snowdon mountain group, the sea, valleys and woodlands, in a walk which is redolent with history and industrial archaeology. It passes Dinas Emrys, where Vortigen, on the run from the Saxons, tried to erect a castle to no avail until a 'boy not of woman born' told him to dig deeper. This he did and he found a lake, and on the side of which a red and white dragon were fighting. Significantly, it was the red dragon which eventually won.

Llangywair is a small hamlet 3 miles south-west of Bala, on the southern side of Llyn Tegid, which is a stop on the Bala Railway with a small picnic site. From the car park go left to Llangywair, and follow the road past Tyddyn Llafar. Passing through forestry plantations, you reach Bwlch y Fwlet, a dilapidated farmhouse. Climb steeply up to the summit of Cefn Gwyn which yields great views of many of the famous mountains of Meirionnydd, the southern part of the National Park. From Cefn Gwyn, walk north-east to a forestry road, and down to the Nant Rhyd Wen stream. Cross the footbridge and follow the road back to Llangywair or take the path that will take you back to the road via Tŷ Cerrig. This 5-mile walk will take approximately three hours.

Llyn Dinas and Lliwedd from the Cwm Bychan walk above Sygun Copper Mine

6 Exploring the Park

The magical scenery of the Dyfi estuary at sunset. The lights on the horizon belong to the seaside village of Borth on the Ceredigion coast

ABERDYFI

It is from here that you can hear 'the Bells of Aberdyfi' as they ring from Cantref Gwaelod, a land of milk and honey lost to the sea when according to legend the gatekeeper, Seithennyn, having enjoyed too much mead perhaps, fell asleep.

Aberdyfi depends for its bread and water today on tourism. It is a small resort village situated on a narrow stretch of land between the southernmost hills of Snowdonia and the saltmarshes and sands of the Dyfi Estuary. Across the estuary (ferries are available) is the nature reserve of Ynyslas run by the RSPB, which offers truly exciting prospects for bird lovers and anyone interested in wildlife.

Aberdyfi was originally an important fishing and harbour village, exporting woollen goods and lead, and it was also a shipbuilding centre. Its importance as an industrial village declined with the coming of the railway in the latter part of the nineteenth century.

The village history is displayed in the information centre on the harbour, which is worth visiting in its own right.

BALA

Y Bala, to give its full name (meaning land between two stretches of water), lies between the Dyfrdwy (River Dee) and Llyn Tegid (Bala Lake). It is a busy tourist centre and serves as a gateway town to Snowdonia. As noted in the main text, it is an old settlement and market town which was given status by the Normans in 1312 with the main street stretching down from the motte and bailey castle site at Tomen y Bala.

The village has a proud history in terms of Welsh culture and politics. In the centre of the town is a statue to Tom Ellis MP who, with Lloyd George, was prominent in establishing a movement for giving Wales its freedom towards the end of the nineteenth century. In May 1999, a hundred years later, his dream began to emerge with the advent of the National Assembly for Wales. A colleague of Tom Ellis, Michael D. Jones, could not wait and he organised a migration to Patagonia to establish a free Welsh colony in the wilds of Argentina. He is also commemorated in the town. Outside Capel Tegid is the statue to Thomas Charles, the founder of the Bible Society.

Bala is still an important local centre for the farming population and you would have to listen very carefully to hear much English spoken on Thursday, which is market day.

There is an information centre at the leisure centre by the lake.

Llyn Tegid and Arenig Fawr, near Bala

BARMOUTH

Barmouth has a similar history to Aberdyfi in that the original settlement was a fishing port and exporter of goods from Dyffryn Mawddach. In contrast to Aberdyfi however, the fishing industry, especially shellfish, is still active. The working port and the old village clinging on to the cliffs are in marked contrast to the funfairs and ice-cream booths of the nineteenth-century resort. Barmouth became the classic seaside resort reached by rail, and the boarding-houses remain in a prominent line inland from the promenade. Also still surviving is the only wooden railway viaduct operational in Wales, and Barmouth Bridge at the mouth of the most beautiful valley in Snowdonia is a feature in its own right.

Dinas Oleu, the cliff rising out of the 'new' town, was the first property bequeathed to the National Trust in 1895. You may lose your breath in getting up there but the short walk along the cliff edge offers excellent panoramas of the estuary mouth and the coastline north towards Harlech. There is an information centre near the station.

BETWS Y COED

Undoubtedly, the top mountain resort centre of Snowdonia. Apparently it was popular for honeymooners in the Victorian age, and it is worth noting that the impressive fronts of the hostelries face north so that the delicate skins of the newly-weds would not be blotched by the sun. The National Park Authority has been following a conservation programme to maintain and/or restore these Victorian façades.

Betws y Coed (the beadhouse in the wood) is a focal centre in the full sense. From the south comes the Conwy itself, joined by the Lledr (and the route from Blaenau Ffestiniog) at Pont yr Afanc (the bridge of the beaver) just outside the village. In the village, the Llugwy hurtles beneath Pont y Pair (the bridge of the cauldron) to create the main Conwy just north of the village. It is no surprise therefore that the main road route from London to Holyhead, the A5, descends into Betws y Coed from the east crossing the Waterloo Bridge before then rising up Dyffryn Llugwy towards Capel Curig and the traverse across the mountains towards Bangor and then Anglesey.

The main hotel is the Royal Oak with its traditional eminence attested by its substantial stables. Today, Y Stablau form the National Park Authority's major information centre, which it operates in partnership with the Forestry Commission and the RSPB as well as the North Wales Tourism Ltd. The FC have a series of walks in the vicinity which are outlined in the centre, and the RSPB exhibition is a great experience for children. But Betws y Coed is not only a summer destination; in the autumn, anglers appear as the rivers that converge on the village are rich in salmon and sewin (sea trout).

BETHESDA

A major quarrying settlement that owes everything to the huge Penrhyn Slate Quarry which dominates it. Like other quarrying settlements, Bethesda is made up of different smaller communities such as Bryn Melyn, Rachub and Caergai, with the amalgamated town taking its name from the most prominent chapel. The lord of the manor, Lord Penrhyn's, influence was all-pervading and you may notice that almost all the pubs of Bethesda are on one side of the road and fairly closely bunched. This is because the lord would not allow taverns on his ground, and so the only part that was not of the Penrhyn Estate became the tavern quarter of Bethesda.

The Lledr valley near Betws y Coed

Bethesda became synonymous with the trade union movement in Britain during the Great Strike of 1900–1903, when 4,000 quarrymen stood out against the landlord but lost the battle and some 2,000 were allowed to return. The war went on, however, and the Penrhyn quarrymen earned an honourable place in the history of trade unionism in Britain.

McAlpines now operate the quarry with about 300 employees, and so even though quarrying is still important, Bethesda (pop. 4,278) is struggling to re-establish itself with a new identity. The A5 runs through the town and the fact that the road has been declared a Historic Route is good news. It has certainly the potential to be a gateway town into Snowdonia as this is the first settlement to be reached after turning off the A55, the main arterial route from the east. Bethesda nestles at the mouth of Nant Ffrancon which leads directly to Cwm Idwal, the Carneddau and Glyder Ranges and to Dyffryn Ogwen.

BEDDGELERT

Beddgelert means 'the grave of Gelert', the faithful hound who lost his head over a prince's baby – if you believe the legend. While it may be a creation of the landlord of the Goat Hotel in the second half of the nineteenth century, it does evoke some of the romance of Snowdonia. When that 'romance' is coupled with good marketing and a commercial brain, you have a tourist industry.

Besides such considerations, Beddgelert is located at the junction of the Colwyn and Glaslyn rivers, before the latter squeezes its way through Aberglaslyn Pass to the open expanse of Traeth Mawr and the sea at Porthmadog.

The village of Beddgelert

The National Trust owns much property in this area and have an interesting information centre and shop by the bridge at Llywelyn House, and an education centre at Craflwyn just outside the village.

Beddgelert is also the home of Gelert Products, which produces mountain ware of world-wide fame, showing what can be done with that commercial brain and utilising local characteristics. Walks along the Welsh Highland Railway and Sygun.

BLAENAU FFESTINIOG

If Bethesda is the quarrying town of slate, Blaenau Ffestiniog (pop. 4,520) is the mining town. Here the extraction has traditionally been underground with the largest site, what was the Oakley Quarry, reaching at least 600ft beneath the town. Across the road from the Ffestiniog Quarry is Llechwedd Quarry, which is well-known as the Slate Caverns tourist attraction. Around 200,000 people visit Llechwedd each year and it is yet another example of the successful adaptation of local resources for a new function.

Blaenau Ffestiniog has not received the full benefit from tourism. Much money has been spent on landscaping the slate waste tips that surround the town and on revitalising the town centre. In 1986, the Ffestiniog Railway 'returned' to the town centre as the line was reopened, and now the Conwy Valley and Ffestiniog lines terminate at the same station. Close to the station is the National Park information centre.

CAERNARFON

Caernarfon (pop. 9,681) has long been an important administrative centre and is now the county town of Gwynedd. However, it is chiefly known for its hugely-impressive Anglo-Norman castle which still dominates the town. This is not the only fortification as Twt Hill is the site of an Iron Age fort and, although little remains, it is still worth a visit if only for the views. In the upper part of Caernarfon is the Roman fort of Segontium, which has a small but interesting museum.

It must not be forgotten that Caernarfon was an important port in the nineteenth century and the Albert Docks remind us that it also built ships. The most famous local ship engineers were the De Wintons, who turned their skills to building trains for the quarries and the Ffestiniog Railway.

Next to the castle is the open area of Y Maes where a statue of Lloyd George seems to defy the imperial walls behind him. Y Maes also hosts a statue of Sir Hugh Owen, a great educationalist of the nineteenth century, as well as a host of buses. If you cannot make head or tail of what you are hearing about you on Y Maes, do not be too concerned because the Cofis of Caernarfon are like the Cockneys of London – they have their own language and customs.

Blaenau Ffestiniog cradled among the Moelwyn mountains

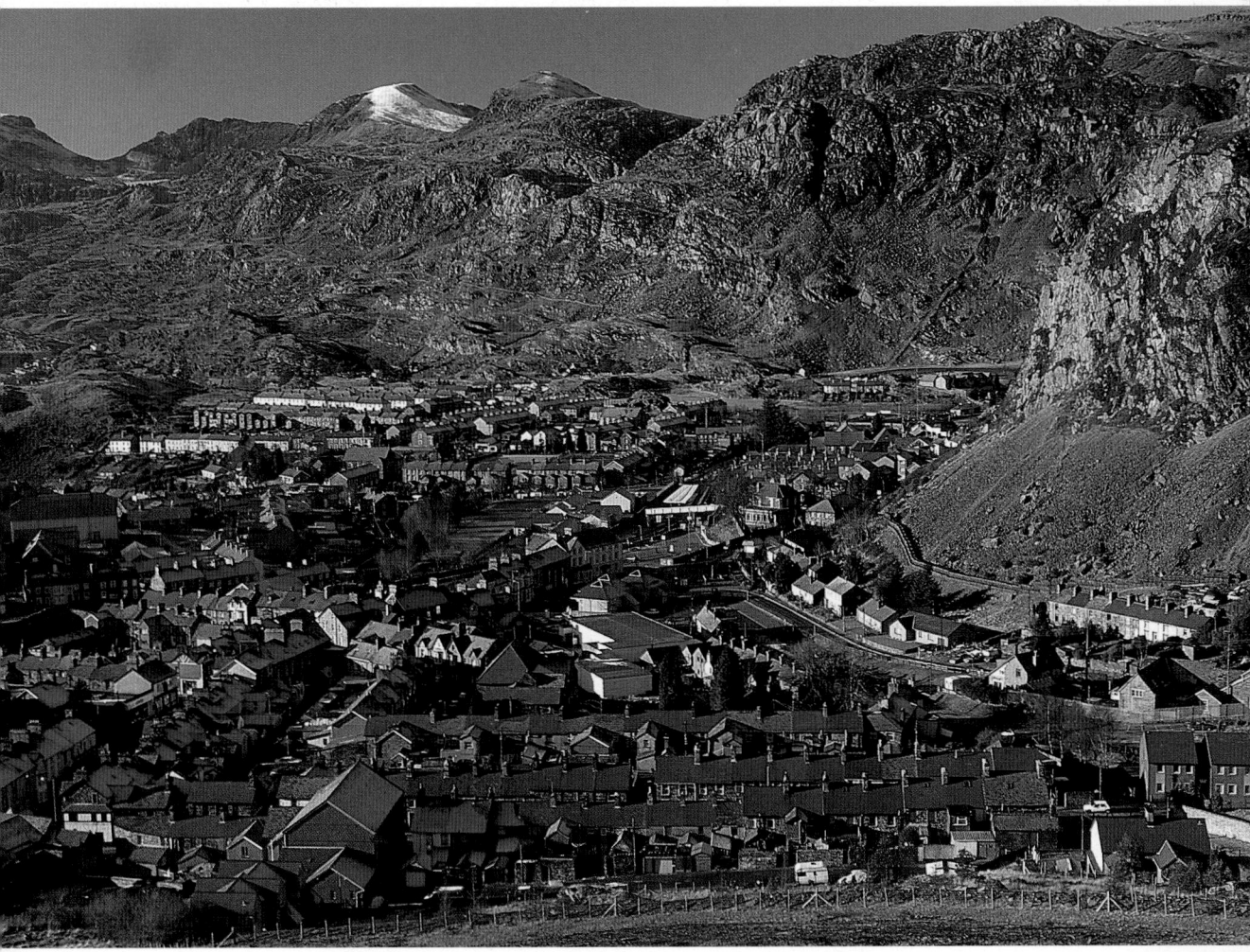

CAPEL CURIG

Capel Curig is scattered around the junction of the A5 and the A4086 where the former veers towards Dyffryn Conwy and the latter heads out over Dyffryn Mymbyr and the most well-known views of the Snowdon Range. It has always been associated with mountain recreation. The Sports Council's Mountain Centre, Plas y Brenin, was originally the Eagle Hotel, built by Lord Penrhyn as a watering hole on his round trips from his home at Penrhyn Castle near Bangor to the mountains. It is not surprising that this little hamlet has two climbing shops and two pubs.

CONWY

Conwy (pop.13,508) is another medieval castle town on the edge of the National Park which contains many features of interest. The castle itself is a slightly smaller version of Caernarfon but links with the walled city are clear. Within the walls are a number of features of varying age, with the late medieval town house of the Wynns of Gwydir, Plas Mawr, recently restores by CADW, an outstanding example of its genre. Another exemplar of its period is Aberconwy House, a merchant's residence of the medieval period, now in the care of the National Trust.

Approaching the town from across the Conwy, you will see the Telford suspension bridge of 1826 complete with crenellated Gothic turrets, and also Stephenson's tubular girder railway bridge. Alongside these is the 1950s road bridge to Conwy and unseen but close at hand is the 1980s Conwy Tunnel for the A55, rushing towards Anglesey.

CORRIS

A slate village that was avoided when the National Park boundary was drawn. If you look at the boundary here you will see that its quite convoluted as it strove to circumvent the slate-scarred areas. Corris is a younger settlement than other slate villages, with the building material being consistently more obvious as slate slabs or in Welsh 'pena' llifia' (sawn ends). The Corris Railway has its base here. On the site of the old Bwlch Coch Quarry is the craft centre, and inside the old quarry is the 'Arthurian Legend Experience'.

Snowdon and Llyn Mymbyr near Capel Curig

Dyffryn Conwy – a valley opened up and widened by glacial forms

Opposite: Dolgellau in its magnificent setting under the summit of Cader Idris

DINAS MAWDDWY

A small village on the south-eastern approach to Snowdonia set in the deep and softer valleys of the Silurian rocks. It had at one time a rail link to Machynlleth to transport slate. The old station buildings now house Meirion Mill, a woollen factory with a café and information shop. From here you can go to Cwm Cywarch and Cwm Mawddwy by car and then by foot to enjoy the steep-sided and tranquil valleys.

DOLGELLAU

Dolgellau has always had pretensions for grandeur. It is certainly set in grand surroundings, with the majestic Cader Idris and the Wnion Valley a worthy small sister to Dyffryn Mawddach. The architecture and the building material are very distinctive and give it an air of granite-like solidarity. In the late eighteenth century it was the centre of the thriving Meirionnydd woollen industry, and many of the grand houses on the northern side of town date from that period. It used to be the county town of Meirionnydd but now houses the area offices for the county of Gwynedd. It once had its own prison, and legend has it that prisoners who managed the slip their fetters could lose their way in the jumble of streets. Historically, Dolgellau and its environs has had strong association with the Society of Friends. Above the town, on the way to Cader, is Bryn Mawr, home of T. Ellis, who went to America and founded what has become a famous girls' college of the same name. This association is reflected in the information centre at Eldon Square, called Tŷ Meirion.

HARLECH

A smaller castle than Caernarfon and Conwy, but still very impressive, perched above the flat coastal plain. Although at one time the sea must have reached the foot of the 'beautiful stone' – the derivation of Harlech from 'hardd lech' – this was not the case when the castle was built, although at that time a canal connected the

castle to the sea. The sea must have reached the castle rock when the giant Bendigeidfran, sitting on the 'hardd lech' with his sister Branwen, first saw Matholwch with his hordes arriving form Ireland to claim Branwen's hand.

Harlech Castle was for a time the base of Owain Glyndwr when he led the rebellion against the English throne from 1400 to 1410.

Below the castle today is the theatre Theatr Ardudwy next to Coleg Harlech, a Workers' Educational College established in 1927 to prepare members of the working class for higher education. Between the town and the sea are the dunes, which contain a golf course and in the more northern reaches, an important National Nature Reserve.

Evening tranquillity on Llyn Padarn, Llanberis

LLANBERIS

Llanberis was originally built to accommodate the workers of the Dinorwig Quarry which still dominates the town even though it has been closed since 1969. The quarry has been taken over by the Dinorwig Hydro Electric Scheme owned by North Wales Hydro which also runs a huge exhibition centre. The workshops of Dinorwig Quarry which had their own foundry are now the North Wales Slate Museum and are well worth a visit. In the same complex is the terminal of the Padarn Railway, which was originally opened in 1828 to carry slate from the quarry to the sea. Close at hand is the Quarry Hospital, kept like the workshop just as they were when the axe fell. But it is difficult to imagine what the hospital would have been like, the workshop without the noise of the machinery, or the quarry without the smell of powder or danger.

LLANRWST

A small market town in the Conwy Valley noted for its arched bridge dating from the seventeenth century. Closely associated with the Gwydir Family, Gwydir Castle itself is close at hand as is Gwydir Chapel, decorated by Robert Wynn, which has a splendid stone coffin, once thought to have contained the remains of the greatest of medieval Welsh monarchs, Llywelyn Fawr. Llywelyn was born in Dolwyddelan and had close associations with Dyffryn Conwy, especially with Maenen Abbey.

PENRHYNDEUDRAETH

When it was built, this was a dormitory village for the Ffestiniog Quarries with the commuting quarrymen using the Ffestiniog Railway for their journey to work. The village, built by David Williams, a local landowner and the first Liberal MP for Merionnydd, is an unusual example in Snowdonia of a designed settlement, as can be seen from the width of the main street. Apart from the quarries, its life blood for a number of generations was the explosives factory. When that closed in the late 1990s at the same time as the Trawsfynydd Nuclear Power Station, the village suffered greatly from the loss of employment and subsequent migration.

But now, as in much of Snowdonia, new ideas are coming through. Part of the old explosives site is a nature reserve and another part is a business park. The people in the village have formed an organisation called Penrhyn 2000 and are putting ideas into action to promote the village and its surroundings.

Traeth Mawr from Cnicht

PORTHMADOG

Porthmadog came into existence following an Act of Parliament in 1821 which gave power to William Alexander Madocks to build the harbour and other facilities. The harbour only became possible after Mr Madocks had erected an embankment across Traeth Mawr, the mouth of the Glaslyn, in 1812. Before that Madocks had begun to erect his ideal harbour town at Tremadog, where the central piazza style 'square' is an outstanding example of urban design. He opened a canal to link Tremadog to the sea but everything changed after the building of the Cob, when the channelling of the river through sluice gates scoured out a deep-water channel. The Cob also made possible the Ffestiniog Railway, which officially opened in 1836 to carry slates from the mountains to the sea. Now the line carries tourists from the sea to the mountain and back again.

Porthmadog is a busy tourist resort village in the summer, with the stations of both the Ffestiniog and Welsh Highland Railways creating much activity. It has a small museum describing its maritime heritage and an information centre. If you are able to wander from the town, walk up Moel y Gest for a wonderful view of the mountains, the estuary, the town and the sea.

TRAWSFYNYDD

This little village has been long identified, of course, with the Nuclear Power Station, which ceased to operate in 1993. In the late 1990s, the huge concrete slab that housed the reactors still stands and the debate goes on about the method of decommissioning. On the site itself there is an excellent information centre and there is a nature trail nearby. The village has formed a community association

Tal y Llyn Lake (Llyn Mwyngil) which lies in the Bala fault line. The valley has been formed by erosion along this line of weakness

called 'Trawsnewid' (changing Trawsfynydd) and is making vigorous efforts to turn the lake and its surroundings into a tourist attraction. In March 1999 a pleasure boat was launched to convey people around the lake.

To Welsh people, Trawsfynydd is associated with the 'Bardd y Gadair Ddu' (the bard of the black chair). The bard was Hedd Wyn, a local farmer who won the National Eisteddfod chair in 1917 but was killed in the trenches of Passchendaele before he could claim his honour. There is a statue of Hedd Wyn in the centre of the village.

TYWYN

Contrary to what most people think, Tywyn is a very old settlement. The church of St Cadfan's was founded in the early medieval period and still retains twelfth-century work in the nave. Much more significantly, the site is the home of the the Stone of Cadfan, which dates to the seventh century and bears the first known example of written Welsh, as opposed to the Brythonic (British), language.

The village itself bears the imprint of local landowner John Corbett, who built many of the larger buildings in the early nineteenth century in anticipation of the tourists who arrived in large numbers with the main line railway. The Talyllyn Railway has its terminus here, and at the station there is also a Narrow Gauge Museum.

Tywyn means the seashore and the sands are worth a visit. It is also possible to walk along the shore to Aberdyfi.

Information

Useful addresses

Snowdonia National Park
Authority
Penrhyndeudraeth, Gwynedd
LL48 6LF
Tel: 01766 770274 Fax: 771211

Countryside Council for Wales
Plas Penrhos, Bangor, Gwynedd
LL57 2LQ
Tel: 01248 385500

CADW
Crown Buildings, Cathays Park,
Cardiff CF1 3NQ
Tel: 01222 826171

National Trust
Trinity House, Llandudno
Tel: 01492 860123

North Wales Wildlife Trust
376, High Street, Bangor,
Gwynedd
Tel: 01248 351541

Snowdonia Society
Tŷ Hyll, Capel Curig, Betws y Coed
Tel: 01690 720287

Campaign for the Protection of
Rural Wales
Tŷ Gwyn, 31 High Street,
Welshpool, Powys
SY21 7YD
Tel: 01938 552525

Major attractions

Chwarel Hen Llanfair
Slate Caverns, Llanfair near
Harlech
Tel: 01766 830306

Llechwedd Slate Caverns
Blaenau Ffestiniog
Tel: 01766 780247

North Wales Slate Museum
Padarn Country Park, Llanberis
Tel: 01286 870630

Sygun Copper Mine
Beddgelert
Tel: 01766 510100

Talyllyn Railway
Wharf Station, Tywyn
Tel: 01654 710472

Llanberis Lake Railway
Padarn Country Park, Llanberis
Tel: 01286 870549

Ffestiniog Railway
Harbour Station, Porthmadog
Tel: 01766 512340

Fairbourne Railway
Fairbourne, Arthog
Tel: 01341 250362

Snowdon Mountain Railway
Llanberis
Tel: 01286 870223

Bala Lake Railway
Llanuwchllyn, Bala
Tel: 01678 540666

Ffestiniog Visitor Centre
Tan y Grisiau,
Blaenau Ffestiniog
Tel: 01766 830465

Electric Mountain
Llanberis
Tel: 01286 870636

Trawfynydd Nuclear Power
Station
Trawsfynydd Lake Visitor Centre,
Trawsfynydd
Tel: 01766 540622

Centre for Alternative Technology
Llywernog, Machynlleth
Tel: 01645 702400

Merthyr Farm
Welsh Hill Farm, Merthyr Farm,
Harlech
Tel: 01766 780344

Portmeirion Village
Portmeirion, Penrhyndeudraeth
Tel: 01766 770228

Celtica
Experience the World of the Celts,
Y Plas, Machynlleth
Tel: 01654 702702

King Arthur's Labyrinth
Corris Craft Centre, Corris
Tel: 01654 761584

Activities

Bala Adventure and Watersports
Centre
Centre Office, Bala Lake
Foreshore, Bala
Tel: 01678 521059

The Rhiw Goch
Dry Ski and Mountain Bike
Centre, Bronaber, Trawsfynydd
Tel: 01766 540578

Dolgellau Angling Association
Maescaled, Dolgellau
Tel: 01341 422706

Tourist Information Centres

Aberdyfi
The Wharf, Aberdyfi LL35 0ED
Tel/Fax: 01654 767321

Y Bala
Leisure Centre, Pensarn Road
Y Bala LL23 7SR
Tel/Fax: 01678 521021

Barmouth
Old Library, Station Road,
Barmouth LL42 1LU
Tel/Fax: 01341 280787

Betws y Coed
Royal Oak Stables, Betws y Coed
LL24 0AH
Tel: 01690 710426 Fax: 710665

Blaenau Ffestiniog
Isallt, High Street, Blaenau
Ffestiniog LL41 3HD
Tel/Fax: 01766 830360

Caernarfon
Oriel Pendeitsh, Castle Street,
Caernarfon Ll55 2NA
Tel: 01286 672232 Fax: 678209

Conwy
CADW Visitor Centre, Castle
Entrance, Conwy
LL32 8LD
Tel: 01492 592248 Fax: 584376

Corris
Craft Centre, Corris, Machynlleth
SY20 9SP
Tel/Fax: 01654 761244

Dolgellau
Tŷ Meirion
Dolgellau LL40 1PU
Tel: 01341 422888 Fax: 422576

Harlech
Gwyddfor House
Harlech LL46 1DR
Tel/Fax: 01766 780658

Llanberis
41a High Street, Llanberis
LL55 4UR
Tel: 01286 870765 Fax: 872141

Porthmadog
High Street, Porthmadog
LL49 9LD
Tel: 01766 512981 Fax: 512247

Tywyn
High Street, Tywyn LL36 9AD
Tel/Fax: 01654 710070

MAPS

The use of excellent appropriate
Ordnance Survey maps is highly
recommended for any detailed
exploration of the National Park,
especially if you are leaving the car
behind and venturing out into the
countryside.

Outdoor Leisure Maps (1:25,000)
No 17 Snowdonia – Snowdon &
Conwy Valley;
No 18 Snowdonia – Harlech,
Portmadog & Bala;
No 23 Snowdonia – Cadair Idris &
Lake Bala
Landrangers (1:50,000)
No 115 Snowdon ;
No 116 Denbigh & Colwyn Bay;
No 124 Dolgellau;
No 125 Bala & Lake Vyrnwy;
No 135 Aberystwyth & Machynlleth

FURTHER READING

Borrow, George. *Wild Wales* (1862,
John Jones Publishing, Rhuthun,
paperback edition, 1998)
Condry, W. *The Snowdonia
National Park* (Collins New
Naturalist, 1966)
Crew, P. and Musson, C.
Snowdonia from the air;
Patterns in the Landscape
(Snowdonia National Park
Authority, 1998)
Davies, J. *The Making of Wales*
(CADW/Allan Sutton, 1996)
Howells, M. F., Leveridge, B. E.,
and Reedman, A. J. *Snowdonia,
Geological Field Guide* (Unwin
Paperbacks,1981)
Lacey, W. S. and Morgan, M. J.
(Eds). *The Nature of North Wales*
(Barracuda Books, 1989)
Lynch, Frances. *Gwynedd, A Guide
to Ancient and Historic Wales*
(CADW/HMSO, 1995)
Morris, J. *Wales, Epic view of a small
country* (Viking, 1998)
Moscati, S., Frey, O., Raftery, B.,
and Szabo, M. *The Celts*
(Thames and Hudson, 1991)
North, F. J., Campbell, Bruce and
Scott, Richenda. *Snowdonia, The
National Park of North Wales*
(Collins New Naturalist, 1949)
Perrin, Jim. *Visions of Snowdonia,
Landscape and Legends* (BBC
Books, 1997)
Rees, Ioan Bowen (Ed). *The
Mountains of Wales, an anthology
in verse and prose* (University of
Wales Press, 1992)
Rhys, John. *Celtic Folklore, Welsh
and Manx* (Reissued from
original 1901 text by Wildwood
House, 1980)
Thomas, R. S. *Collected Poems,
1945–1990* (Phoenix Giants,
1993)

Index

Page numbers in *italics* indicate illustrations